THE
IMPOSTOR'S DAUGHTER

THE
IMPOSTOR'S DAUGHTER

A ^{TRUE} Memoir

Laurie Sandell

Little, Brown and Company
New York Boston London

Little, Brown and Company
Hachette Book Group
237 Park Avenue, New York, NY 10017
Visit our Web site at www.HachetteBookGroup.com

First Edition: July 2009

Little, Brown and Company is a division of Hachette Book Group, Inc. The Little, Brown name and logo are trademarks of Hachette Book Group, Inc.

Color by Paige Pooler

Library of Congress Cataloging-in-Publication Data
Sandell, Laurie.
  The impostor's daughter : a true memoir / Laurie Sandell
    p. cm.
  ISBN 978-0-316-03305-3
1. Sandell, Laurie—Comic books, strips, etc. 2. Journalists—United States—Biography—Comic books, strips, etc. 3. Graphic novels. I. Title.
  PN4874.S2687A3 2009
  070.92—dc22   2008034091
[B]

10 9 8 7 6 5 4 3 2 1

Printed in China

For all the
truth tellers

SECRETS

WHENEVER MY FATHER WENT OUT OF TOWN, HE HAD THE MAIL STOPPED.
IT DIDN'T MATTER IF HE WAS GONE FOR ONE, TWO, OR TEN DAYS —
IF MY FATHER WASN'T HOME, THE MAIL DIDN'T COME.

I WONDERED WHAT MADE HIM
GUARD THE MAIL SO JEALOUSLY.
HIS EXPLANATIONS DIDN'T
MAKE SENSE.

ACH, IT'S ALL
JUNK MAIL,
SEE?

STONEMAN
COLLEGE
BOOKSTORE

BUT THERE
IS NO
"STONEMAN
COLLEGE."

A-**HA**!
I KNOW THAT, AND
YOU KNOW THAT,
BUT **THEY** DON'T
KNOW THAT.

THE FEW TIMES I MANAGED TO INTERCEPT THE MAIL, I FOUND THAT EVERY LETTER IN THE PILE WAS ADDRESSED TO A DIFFERENT NAME.

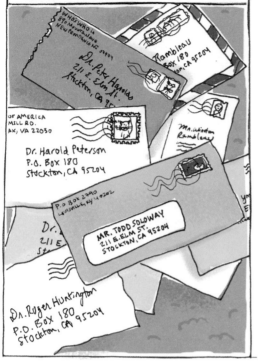

EVERY NOW AND THEN, THESE STRANGE NAMES WOULD POP UP ON THE OTHER END OF THE PHONE.

IS WINSTON RAMBLEAU THERE?

WRONG NUMBER.

LATER THAT NIGHT...

WHO CALLED? THAT WAS FOR ME, DAMMIT!

AFTER THAT, WHATEVER NAME THEY GAVE, I JUST YELLED FOR MY DAD.

IT'S FOR YOU!

I GREW UP IN CALIFORNIA IN A HOUSE AT THE END OF A CUL-DE-SAC ON A WIDE, SMOOTH STREET. I WAS THE OLDEST OF THREE GIRLS.

FROM THE OUTSIDE, OUR HOUSE LOOKED PRETTY MUNDANE.

NOT SO ON THE INSIDE.

4

MY FATHER WAS A PROFESSOR OF ECONOMICS AT THE UNIVERSITY OF THE PACIFIC IN STOCKTON, CALIFORNIA. I WOULD GO TO CLASS WITH HIM ON OCCASION AND SIT IN THE BACK ROW WHILE HE PACED IN FRONT OF THE LECTERN, STOPPING EVERY FEW MINUTES TO WIPE HIS SWEATY FOREHEAD WITH A FOLDED HANDKERCHIEF.

ANGRY ARGENTINE DNA

CLEARLY YOU ARE NOT FAMILIAR WITH THE MATERIAL!

HIS STUDENTS SEEMED TERRIFIED OF HIM, BUT TO ME HE JUST LOOKED STRONG AND HANDSOME — LIKE AN ITALIAN TENOR — WITH HIS GENEROUS GUT AND HIS THICK BLACK HAIR SWEPT INTO A POMPADOUR.

DURING MIDTERMS, I KEPT MY FATHER COMPANY AT THE KITCHEN TABLE WHILE HE GRADED EXAMS.

YOU SEE HOW THIS STUDENT CHOSE THE CORRECT ANSWER, THEN CHANGED HIS MIND?

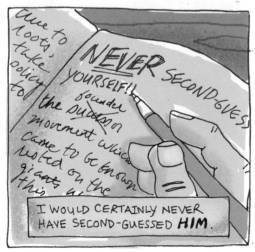

I WOULD CERTAINLY NEVER HAVE SECOND-GUESSED *HIM*.

5

HE MAINTAINED A LIBRARY OF ELEVEN THOUSAND BOOKS. HE'D READ THEM ALL. ANYTHING I WANTED TO KNOW ABOUT, HE SIMPLY WALKED OVER TO A SHELF, PULLED A BOOK DOWN, THEN FLIPPED IT OPEN THE EXACT PAGE THAT SHOWED HIS POINT.

THIS ONE.

BUT HE WASN'T JUST BOOK SMART. HE WAS A BONA FIDE GENIUS.

IT'S AN ORGANIZATION CALLED MENSA, AND YES, YOUR FATHER IS A MEMBER. BY QUITE A FEW POINTS.

HE'D GRADUATED NUMBER ONE IN HIS CLASS FROM THE UNIVERSITY OF BUENOS AIRES.

THE STUPIDEST THING I EVER DID WAS SELL THAT MEDAL. IT WAS SOLID GOLD.

IF YOU EVER GET IT BACK, CAN I HAVE IT?

HE'D GOTTEN A LAW DEGREE FROM NYU, A PHD FROM COLUMBIA, AND HAD TAUGHT AT STANFORD.

WRITTEN POSITION PAPERS FOR KISSINGER.

SAT ON THE NATIONAL SECURITY COUNCIL.

HE COULD ALSO IDENTIFY EVERY PIECE OF CLASSICAL MUSIC THAT EXISTED.

7

WHERE ALL THIS TALENT CAME FROM, I HAD NO IDEA. MY FATHER WAS ESTRANGED FROM HIS ENTIRE FAMILY. WHEN PRESSED, HE SPOKE OF THEM WITH VENOM — PARTICULARLY HIS STEPSISTER, ELSA, WHOM HIS FATHER ADOPTED AFTER MARRYING HER MOTHER.

SHE WAS **HORRIBLE.** A WITCH.

THE ONE EXCEPTION WAS HIS LATE FATHER — A STRICT, GERMAN TASKMASTER — WHOM HE WORSHIPPED.

HE WAS A TWENTY-FOUR-HOUR TEACHING MACHINE. BY THE TIME I WAS YOUR AGE, I KNEW EVERY CAPITAL OF EVERY COUNTRY IN THE WORLD.

WHEN I WAS FIVE I STARTED PIANO LESSONS. MY FATHER OFTEN STOOD IN THE DOORWAY, LISTENING. IF I PLAYED A SCALE PERFECTLY, HIS PRAISE WAS SO EFFUSIVE I WANTED TO TAKE A BATH IN IT.

I SWEAR TO GOD, BEETHOVEN COULDN'T HAVE PLAYED THAT SCALE BETTER.

WHEN HE WAS SIMPLY SILENT, I KNEW I'D LET HIM DOWN.

HE WAS LIKE ONE OF THOSE AVUN-CULAR RUSSIAN GYMNASTICS COACHES I'D SEEN ON TV DURING THE OLYMPICS:

POST-PIANO RECITAL

THAT LITTLE JAPANESE KID WAS ABSOLUTELY **BRILLIANT**.

PROGRAM

HOISTING THEIR CHARGES INTO THE AIR WHEN THEY'D COMPLETED A FEAT OF GYM-NASTIC PERFECTION.

TURNING AWAY WHEN THEY'D FAILED.

MY MOTHER TRIED TO MAKE UP FOR MY FATHER'S JUDGMENTS.

YOU'VE NEVER PLAYED THE THIRD MOVEMENT BETTER, I SWEAR.

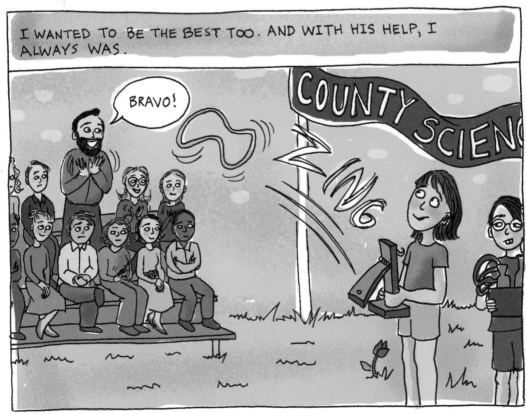

Stories and Gifts

AS EARLY AS KINDERGARTEN, I REMEMBER MY FATHER TRAVELING, SOMETIMES FOR MONTHS AT A TIME. HE RARELY GAVE US NOTICE.

DADDY'S GOING ON A BUSINESS TRIP.

I WANT MARACAS!

SO WE COULD COMMUNICATE WITH HIM WHILE HE WAS AWAY, MY FATHER SET UP HAM RADIO EQUIPMENT, WHICH WAS ALWAYS ON, IN THE DEN.

CRACKLE CRACKLE CRACKLE CRACKLE

I WOULD BE SITTING ON THE COUCH, WATCHING TV, AND THE CRACKLING WOULD GROW LOUDER, PUNCTUATED BY MY FATHER'S DEEP, GRAVELLY BARITONE.

N-TWO-FSD, N-TWO-FSD **COME IN**, N-TWO-FSD.

DAD?

I AM NOT "**DAD**!" I AM **WTXR**!

HE WOULD RETURN AS SUDDENLY AS HE'D LEFT.

DADDY!!!

BEARING THE PROMISED GIFTS.

WHATEVER PAIN I HAD FELT IN MY FATHER'S ABSENCE VANISHED THE MINUTE HE FLIPPED OPEN THE LID OF THAT SUITCASE.

THAT NIGHT AT DINNER...

WHAT WAS PANAMA LIKE?

IT WAS VERY WET—AND THE HEAT WAS HORRENDOUS. THE MOSQUITOES, I SWEAR TO YOU, SOME OF THEM WERE THE SIZE OF YOUR HAND.

HE TOLD US ABOUT THE WOODEN HOUSES OF THE SHANTYTOWNS, WHICH CLUNG TO THE SIDE OF A MOUNTAIN.

ABOUT A TRIP HE'D TAKEN IN A MOTORIZED CANOE, AFTER WHICH HE'D HIKED THROUGH WAIST-DEEP MUD TO A HIDDEN LOCATION.

HOW HE'D SEEN JEWELS THAT SPARKLED LIKE MERCURY, AND ONE TEARDROP-SHAPED STONE AS BIG AS THE HOPE DIAMOND.

JUST LIKE THAT, HE WAS BACK IN OUR LIVES.

MORE!

SHH... TOMORROW.

13

WHEN I WAS SIX I FOUND A VELVET CASE IN A BOX IN THE ATTIC.

I CARRIED THE CASE DOWNSTAIRS TO MY FATHER, AND HE GREW MISTY-EYED.

THAT LED TO HOURS OF THE MOST RIVETING STORIES I'D EVER HEARD.

BULLETS WERE COMING FROM EVERYWHERE— ALL OF A SUDDEN, SOMEBODY YELLS, **GRENADE!**

OVER THE NEXT FEW DAYS, WE DISAPPEARED INTO THE DEN FOR CONVERSATIONS THAT LASTED FOR HOURS.

DO YOU WANT HER TO REPEAT THESE STORIES AT SCHOOL?

AY, LEAVE US BE FOR JUST TEN **MINUTES**!

I WON'T.

HOURS LATER...

I DON'T KNOW IF THEY HAD ORDERS TO BUMP ME OR NOT—BUT I MADE IT ALIVE TO LA PAZ.

THERE WERE SO MANY STORIES. I WANTED TO HEAR THEM ALL.

THE MAN SAID, "LADIES AND GENTLEMEN, I HAVE THE PAINFUL DUTY TO INFORM YOU THAT DOÑA MARIA EVA DUARTE DE PERÓN HAS DIED. I JUMPED TEN FEET IN THE AIR AND YELLED, **THE WHORE IS DEAD! THE WHORE IS DEAD!** MY COUSIN RUTH GRABBED MY ARM, BUT IT WAS TOO LATE: I ENDED UP IN PRISON.

I WAS PROUD TO BE THE DAUGHTER OF SUCH A BRAVE MAN.

THE WHORE IS DEAD!

EVERY ONCE IN A WHILE, MY FATHER WOULD GIVE ME A GIFT, A SPECIAL TREASURE.

THIS WOODEN SWORD IS MORE THAN TWO HUNDRED YEARS OLD.

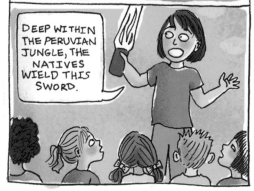

THE NEXT DAY, I WOULD BRING THESE PRESENTS TO SCHOOL FOR SHOW-AND-TELL.

DEEP WITHIN THE PERUVIAN JUNGLE, THE NATIVES WIELD THIS SWORD.

15

PEOPLE CELEBRATE THE IMAGINATION OF A CHILD, BUT I FOUND MY CLASSMATES' OBSERVATIONS TO BE WHOLLY UNINSPIRING.

EVEN THEN, I WAS DRAWN TO COMPELLING, LARGER-THAN-LIFE PERSONALITIES.

VISIONS

WHEN I TURNED SEVEN, MY MOTHER ENROLLED ME IN THE BROWNIES. I WAS GIVEN A LIGHT BROWN JUMPER, A CRISP WHITE SHIRT, AND A DARK BROWN BEANIE.

HMMM...

A FEW DAYS LATER...

THIS IS A FITNESS LIFESTYLE BADGE. THIS IS A YEAR PIN.

I THINK YOU HAVE TO **EARN** THESE.

SALVATION ARMY

AY, **HIJA**, YOU **DID** EARN THEM.

THE AWARDS GLEAMED ON MY CHEST. MY FATHER GAZED AT ME PROUDLY. IN THE MIRROR I SAW A BROWNIE WHO HAD PASSED EVERY TEST, ACCOMPLISHED EVERY GOAL. PERHAPS I **HAD** EARNED THEM.

AROUND THAT TIME, I STARTED DRAWING CARTOONS. MY MATERNAL GRANDFATHER, WHO LIKED TO PAINT AND SKETCH, TAUGHT ME HOW.

MY FIRST DRAWINGS WERE PEACEFUL INTERPRETATIONS OF RURAL LIFE. *

BUT SOON, I WAS ON TO DARKER TABLEAUX, CARTOONS I DREW EXCLUSIVELY FOR MY FATHER. IN EACH DRAWING, HIS HEAD WAS HUGE; OUTRAGEOUSLY OUT OF PROPORTION TO THE REST OF HIS BODY. FOR COMIC FLOURISH, I ADDED A GIANT WART ON THE TIP OF HIS NOSE.

* ACTUAL DRAWINGS.

18

WHEN FINISHED, I WOULD PROP THE CARTOON ON A STATUE CALLED **VISIONS** THAT MY PARENTS KEPT ON A CREDENZA IN THE HALLWAY.

HIDING BEHIND THE BASEMENT DOOR, I'D WAIT FOR MY FATHER TO FIND IT. SOMETIMES I HAD TO WAIT FOR LONG PERIODS.

EVENTUALLY, I'D HEAR HIS FOOT-STEPS IN THE HALL, FAINT AT FIRST, THEN LOUDER. THE HAMMERING IN MY HEART WOULD QUICKEN WITH EVERY STEP.

PRICELESS. THIS IS PRICELESS.

HE SEEMED TO RELISH MY INSIGHTS, PARTICULARLY WHEN THEY WERE AT HIS EXPENSE.

HE'D TAKE THE NEWEST DRAWING AND ADD IT TO A RAPIDLY GROWING PILE IN AN ORANGE CARDBOARD BOX. EVENTUALLY, THERE WERE MORE THAN TWO HUNDRED OF THEM. THEY SAT IN THE ATTIC, COLLECTING DUST. I CONTINUED TO DRAW.

A SURPRISE MOVE

ONE DAY, MY FATHER CAME HOME AND CALLED A FAMILY MEETING. WE ASSEMBLED IN THE DEN. MY MOTHER SAT ON THE SOFA, HOLDING MY THREE-YEAR-OLD SISTER, SYLVIE. KARYN AND I SHARED THE HASSOCK.

WE'RE MOVING TO NEW YORK.

HOORAY!

ONE MINUTE, IT SEEMED, WE WERE PLAYING OUTSIDE, CATCHING FIREFLIES IN JARS.

THE NEXT WE WERE PULLING INTO MY AUNT'S DRIVEWAY.

22

A FEW WEEKS LATER, WE MOVED INTO THE TOP FLOOR OF A
TWO-FAMILY HOUSE ON AN UNREMARKABLE STREET.

MY SISTERS AND I ALL SHARED
A ROOM, AND KARYN AND
SYLVIE SCRAMBLED TO DO MY
BIDDING.

THERE WAS AN UNSPOKEN RULE
IN OUR FAMILY: EVERYONE IN
THE HOUSE SERVED MY FATHER,
AND MY SISTERS SERVED ME.

MY FATHER REINFORCED MY BELIEF THAT I DESERVED TO BE RUNNING A MINI-EMPIRE.

WHICH ONE IS BETTER?

THAT ONE.

ONLY I KNEW THE REAL REASON WHY.

YES, YOU'RE MY FAVORITE. BUT THAT'S JUST BETWEEN US, *CAPISCE*?

ABOUT A MONTH AFTER WE MOVED, MY FATHER STARTED HIS NEW JOB AS A PROFESSOR AT A LOCAL COLLEGE.

THE MONEY IS MUCH BETTER, BUT THIS PLACE IS NO STANFORD. THE LEVEL OF INTELLECT— *NIGHT* AND *DAY*.

HE HIRED A SECRETARY NAMED GIULIA TO WORK IN HIS OFFICE. GIULIA SAT AT ONE OF THE DESKS, MANNING THE PHONE, AND MY FATHER SAT AT THE OTHER, GRADING PAPERS AND TYPING UP MEMOS.

I ADORED GIULIA. SHE SPOKE IN THE HIGH-PITCHED VOICE OF A LITTLE GIRL, SMELLED OF LOVE'S BABY SOFT PERFUME, AND WORE HER HAIR LONG, IN RIPPLING BLACK WAVES.

I DREW HER OFTEN — SHE WAS SOMETHING OF A MUSE.

ABOUT ONCE A MONTH, GIULIA CAME TO OUR HOUSE TO TAKE MY SISTERS AND ME TO DINNER, A MOVIE, OR AN AMUSEMENT PARK.

GIULIA IS HERE!

SHE BOUGHT US WHATEVER WE WANTED — AND WE TOOK FULL ADVANTAGE OF HER GENEROSITY.

Playland

THAT ONE!

25

WE'D RETURN HOME LADEN WITH GIFTS AND BRIMMING WITH STORIES.

SHE LETS US EAT COTTON CANDY BEFORE DINNER— WHY WON'T **YOU?**

AS FAR AS I COULD TELL, MY MOTHER WASN'T THE LEAST BIT CONCERNED ABOUT GIULIA'S CLOSE RELATIONSHIP WITH HER CHILDREN.

WOW, SHE BOUGHT YOU THAT TOO?

THOUGH I SEEM TO HAVE BEEN DISTURBED ON HER BEHALF.

TO MY ARTHRITIS-STRICKEN MOTHER

SIGNS

ONE DAY, MY FATHER ASKED IF I WANTED TO GO INTO THE CITY.

ARE YOU READY TO SEE NEW YORK?

YES!

I WANT TO GO TOO.

MY FATHER AND I WENT TO THE UNITED NATIONS. I WAS IMPRESSED BY THE PHOTOS OF AMBASSADORS THAT LINED THE LONG HALLWAYS.

AT LUNCHTIME, WE ATE IN THE DELEGATES DINING ROOM.

SHE'S TWELVE, OF COURSE?

OF COURSE.

TEN YEARS OLD

AN AMBASSADOR WAS EATING LUNCH JUST A FEW TABLES AWAY.

YOU SEE THAT ELEGANT-LOOKING MAN IN THE SUIT? THAT'S AMBASSADOR YOUSEF MAHMOUD OF BURUNDI.

MY FATHER LIFTED HIS WATER GLASS IN THE MAN'S DIRECTION.

WE ENDED THE DAY WITH A MOVIE AT RADIO CITY MUSIC HALL AND A CARRIAGE RIDE AROUND CENTRAL PARK. I LEANED AGAINST MY FATHER'S SCRATCHY SHIRT AND FELT MY EYES START TO CLOSE. AS LONG AS HE WAS THERE, I FELT SAFE.

A FEW WEEKS LATER, MY FATHER CALLED US INTO THE LIVING ROOM FOR ANOTHER FAMILY MEETING.

I'M LEAVING MY TEACHING POSITION TO PURSUE SOME PERSONAL VENTURES.

THE LIBERALS AT SCHOOL HATE DADDY BECAUSE HE'S A CONSERVATIVE.

I DIDN'T KNOW WHAT A CONSERVATIVE WAS, BUT I HAD HEARD MY FATHER SAY THE WORD ENOUGH TO KNOW THAT THEY — LIKE THE JEWS — WERE THE CHOSEN PEOPLE.

I HAD A VAGUE VISION OF A GROUP OF BLAND, NONDESCRIPT MEN OUT TO GET MY FATHER.

LIBERAL LIBERAL LIBERAL LIBERAL

WE MOVED AGAIN, TO A BIG FOUR-BEDROOM HOUSE IN BRONXVILLE, ONE TOWN AWAY FROM MY AUNT.

IN THE NEW HOUSE, YOU'LL HAVE YOUR OWN ROOM. TRUST ME — IT'S EVEN BETTER.

DAD **ALWAYS** MAKES US MOVE!

MY MOTHER RETURNED TO WORK AS A FIRST-GRADE TEACHER, DRIVING OFF EACH MORNING IN HER WHITE FORD TAURUS.

MY FATHER WAS THERE TO TAKE CARE OF US INSTEAD. HE SPENT MOST OF HIS TIME SPRUCING UP OUR NEW HOME.

AND TALKING TO US ABOUT DEALS HE HAD IN THE WORKS.

IF I SELL THIS TECHNOLOGY IN A PERIOD OF TWO YEARS, I WILL GET TEN PERCENT OF THE SALE. SO WHAT'S TEN PERCENT OF A HUNDRED MILLION DOLLARS? **RIIIGHT.**

BUT UNLIKE MY FRIENDS' FATHERS, HE DIDN'T GO TO WORK. HE SLEPT UNTIL NOON AND DIDN'T BOTHER TO GET DRESSED, WEARING HIS BOXER SHORTS AND AN UNDERSHIRT ALL DAY LONG.

WHAT TIME IS IT?

ALMOST ONE O'CLOCK!

I MADE EGGS.

SOMETIMES HE FELL INTO A BLACK, UNREACHABLE HOLE FOR THE DAY.

LOOK, I MADE YOU— WHAT'S WRONG?

I'M A **FAILURE.**

WHEN I TURNED TWELVE, SOMETHING CHANGED IN OUR RELATIONSHIP.

WHERE...IS...MY... STAPLER?!

I DIDN'T KNOW WHAT I'D DONE TO MAKE HIM SO ANGRY, OR HOW I'D LOST MY IMMUNITY IN THE HOUSEHOLD.

BILL— TAKE IT TO THE BASEMENT!

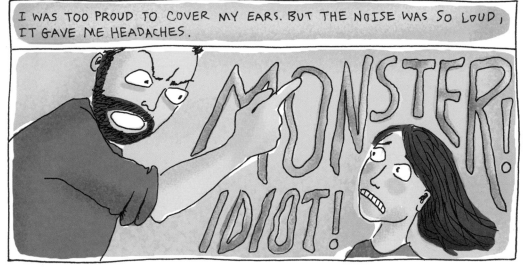

I WAS TOO PROUD TO COVER MY EARS. BUT THE NOISE WAS SO LOUD, IT GAVE ME HEADACHES.

MONSTER! IDIOT!

ONCE WE WENT DOWNSTAIRS, MY MOTHER SEEMED NOT TO HEAR IT AT ALL, THOUGH I COULD STILL HEAR HER MUSIC; IT WAS A SOUNDTRACK TO OUR FIGHTS.

AFTERWARD, I ALWAYS APOLOGIZED. I KNEW I'D SOMEHOW PROVOKED MY FATHER — AND I DIDN'T HAVE HIS STAMINA FOR HOLDING A GRUDGE.

I'M SORRY!

YOU KNOW I ONLY YELL AT YOU BECAUSE WE'RE SO ALIKE.

Magnum P.I.

WERE WE ALIKE? I LIKED TO THINK SO.

OF COURSE I CAN HELP YOU! I'VE READ ALL THE CLASSICS: IVANHOE, TWENTY THOUSAND LEAGUES UNDER THE SEA, ANNA KARENINA.

THE SCARLET LETTER HAWTHORNE

LATER THAT DAY...

HERE YOU GO.

BUT... I CAN'T HAND THIS IN. I'M SUPPOSED TO DO IT MYSELF.

ETHICS AND VIRTUE IN HAWTHORNE'S MASTERPIECE BY LAURIE SANDELL

THEN WHY DID YOU ASK FOR MY HELP?!

33

FOR THE MOST PART HE STAYED OUT OF THE WAY, ALONE, LOCKED IN HIS BEDROOM WITH THE TELEVISION ON AT FULL BLAST. BUT HE HAD ONE RITUAL YOU COULD SET YOUR WATCH BY.

EVERY DAY, HE WOULD LISTEN FOR THE SOUND OF THE MAILTRUCK PULLING INTO OUR DRIVEWAY. THEN HE WOULD RACE DOWNSTAIRS TO THE FRONT DOOR, GRAB A THICK STACK OF LETTERS, AND LOCK HIMSELF IN THE DEN.

M.A.S.H. WILL BE RIGHT BACK AFTER THESE MESSAGES. . .

THROUGH THE SLATS IN THE DOOR, I COULD SEE HIM SLICE THROUGH THE ENVELOPES WITH SURGICAL PRECISION.

AFTER, HE WOULD BRING DOZENS OF LETTERS INTO THE KITCHEN AND THROW THEM IN THE GARBAGE, STEPPING INTO THE CAN AND BOUNCING UP AND DOWN ON ONE FOOT UNTIL THE MAIL WAS SMASHED FLAT.

AND TAKE THE BAG TO THE CURB.

I KNEW MY FATHER WAS STRANGE, NOT LIKE OTHER DADS I KNEW.

BUT MOST OF THE TIME, I THOUGHT THEY WERE STRANGE AND WE WERE THE NORMAL ONES.

DAMMIT, I TOLD YOU NOT TO CHANGE THE CHANNEL!

BY THE TIME I WAS IN HIGH SCHOOL, THOUGH, I KNEW JUST HOW DIFFERENT WE WERE. I RARELY BROUGHT FRIENDS HOME. I COULDN'T RISK IT.

JESUS, DAD, WILL YOU PUT ON SOME CLOTHES?!?

WHAT— I CAN'T BE COMFORTABLE IN MY **OWN HOME**?

THE AIR WAS THICK WITH NEGATIVITY. KARYN AND I, WHO'D NEVER SO MUCH AS BICKERED, STARTED TO HAVE MASSIVE FIGHTS.

BASKIN ROBBINS

THOSE ARE **MINE**!

HELP! HELP!

MY FATHER REPLACED THE LOCKS ON THE DOORKNOBS WITH COMBINATION LOCKS — ON THE **OUTSIDE** OF OUR DOORS.

IS THAT SO YOU CAN LOCK US IN?

DON'T BE RIDICULOUS— IT'S SO YOU CAN'T STEAL EACH OTHER'S CLOTHES.

THERE WAS NO PRIVACY, NO BOUNDARIES.

OH! SORRY.

DAD!

MY FATHER BECAME APOPLECTIC WHEN HE CAUGHT ME WATCHING A MADONNA VIDEO, AND BANNED MTV FROM OUR HOME.

I WILL **NOT** TOLERATE THIS **FILTH** IN MY HOUSE!

IT'S JUST "LIKE A VIRGIN"!

HE WROTE AN ESSAY IN SYLVIE'S NAME AND PUBLISHED IT IN HER SIXTH GRADE LITERARY MAGAZINE. SHE FOUND OUT ONLY WHEN A CLASSMATE COMPLIMENTED HER ON HER WRITING SKILLS.

SHATTERED GLASS AND A FEW BROKEN PIECES BY SYLVIE SANDELL. NOTE: MY DADDY HELPED ME WRITE THIS STORY.

I'M NEVER GOING BACK— **EVER**!!!

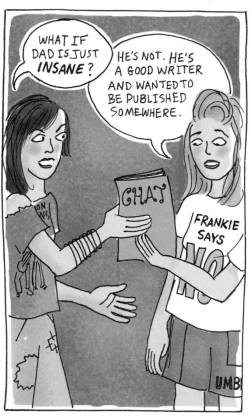

WHAT IF DAD IS JUST **INSANE**?

HE'S NOT. HE'S A GOOD WRITER AND WANTED TO BE PUBLISHED SOMEWHERE.

GHAT

FRANKIE SAYS

LATER THAT DAY...

WHAT DOES HE EVEN **DO** WITH HIS LIFE?

I TOLD YOU: HE SETS UP COMPUTER SYSTEMS FOR FOREIGN GOVERNMENTS.

BUT WHAT DOES THAT MEAN?

DEALS! HE IS MAKING DEALS. NOW STOP ASKING.

I DID STOP ASKING. I TRIED TO CREATE A NORMAL EXISTENCE OUTSIDE MY HOME: DATING THE STAR OF THE BASKETBALL TEAM, ATTENDING MY JUNIOR PROM WITH A NICE JEWISH BOY.

Laurie and date, Gordon Stein 6-2-88

IT DIDN'T WORK. BY MY SENIOR YEAR OF HIGH SCHOOL, I COULDN'T WAIT TO GET AWAY FROM HIM.

KNOCK. KNOCK. KNOCK.

WHAT.

KARYN WAS PLANNING HER OWN ESCAPE: SHE APPLIED EARLY ADMISSION TO THE U.S. NAVAL ACADEMY AND GOT IN.

SIX-MINUTE MILE.

BUT THEN MY FATHER AND I WOULD FALL INTO ONE OF OUR MARATHON LATE-NIGHT CONVERSATIONS, AND HE WOULD TELL ME THINGS HE'D NEVER EVEN TOLD MY MOTHER, AND I WOULD FEEL CLOSE TO HIM AGAIN.

MY FATHER HAD SEVERAL HORSES, SERVANTS— NOW THIS WAS A MAN WHO KNEW HOW TO **LIVE**. MY MOTHER WAS A LITTLE... YOU KNOW, CUCKOO. SHE ONCE PEED ON THE SIDEWALK AFTER SHE DRANK TOO MUCH AT A PARTY.

OTHER SECRETS CAME OUT. I LEARNED MY FATHER HAD CHANGED HIS LAST NAME FROM SCHMIDT TO SANDELL.

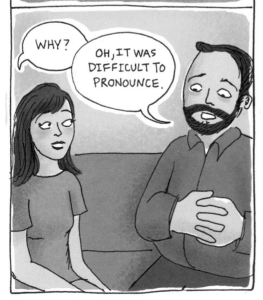

WHY?

OH, IT WAS DIFFICULT TO PRONOUNCE.

WHEN I WAS EIGHTEEN, I LEARNED MY GRANDFATHER HAD KILLED HIMSELF. MY MOTHER SLIPPED— SHE HADN'T MEANT TO TELL ME.

BUT WHY WOULD YOU **KEEP** THAT FROM ME?

BECAUSE IT'S PAINFUL, DARLING.

I LOVED HIM WITH INTENSITY. I HATED HIM WITH INTENSITY. THERE WAS NO MIDDLE GROUND.

40

A DISCOVERY

6573 8225
MEMBER SINCE 1984
LAURIE M. SANDE

NOVEMBER 1992

ONE THANKSGIVING, I CAME HOME FROM COLLEGE TO FIND THAT MY FATHER HAD TURNED MY BEDROOM INTO AN OFFICE.

HE'D COVERED AN ENTIRE WALL WITH HAM RADIO EQUIPMENT, WHICH LOOKED LIKE THE INSIDE OF A SUBMARINE, COMPLETE WITH BLINKING LIGHTS, KNOBS, DIALS, ANTENNAE, AND MICROPHONES.

PRINTS BY MIRÓ AND PICASSO— OR SO HE SAID—WERE STACKED UP AGAINST ONE WALL. HIS LATEST CLAIM WAS THAT HE'D TAKEN UP ART DEALING, BUT MY HUNCH WAS THAT HE WAS IN THE CIA.

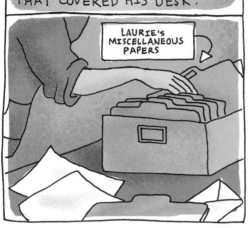

ON THE LAST DAY OF MY VISIT, I PEEKED AT THE FILES THAT COVERED HIS DESK.

LAURIE'S MISCELLANEOUS PAPERS

?

EUROPE TRIP!!!

When I get up to go to the bathroom, Matt stays warm, like a heater. Then he falls asleep again, all warm and cozy, and I think I've I really only known for two weeks? Time Brugge seems to stand no... we are planning the famed garden train to Amst... hope u

cont

WHEN MY FATHER GOT HOME FROM THE GYM, I POUNCED.

YOU PHOTOCOPIED MY *DIARY*?!

42

43

I RETURNED TO SCHOOL AND JOINED A SORORITY. IT WAS THE MOST NORMAL THING I COULD THINK OF TO DO.

AT TWENTY-ONE, I LOST MY VIRGINITY, TO A DISTANT, BEAUTIFUL COMPOSER. HE WAS THE POLAR OPPOSITE OF MY FATHER, SO I HAD NO IDEA HOW TO REACH HIM.

UM... DID YOU SLEEP OK?

AFTER COLLEGE, I HAD A TORTUROUS BREAKUP WITH THE COMPOSER AND MOVED BACK HOME. NOT MUCH HAD CHANGED: MY FATHER STILL SAT AROUND IN HIS UNDERWEAR, WAITED FOR THE MAIL, AND LOCKED HIMSELF IN HIS OFFICE WITH THE TELEVISION AT FULL BLAST.

WHAT?

NOTHING.

ONE SATURDAY I HAPPENED TO CATCH THE MAILMAN FIRST.

I'D NEVER HAD A CREDIT CARD BEFORE. I HAD NO IDEA THEY JUST SENT THEM TO YOU. I DECIDED I'D USE IT TO BUY A MOUNTAIN BIKE.

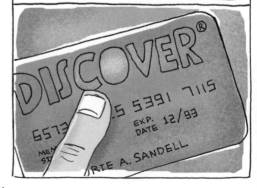

44

LATER, I FOUND MY DAD IN THE KITCHEN. HE WAS LOOKING THROUGH THE REFRIGERATOR FOR HIS "POTION," A MIXTURE OF FRUIT JUICE AND SODA.

I WAS FURIOUS BECAUSE I REALLY WANTED THE MOUNTAIN BIKE, NOT BECAUSE I SUSPECTED HE'D DONE SOMETHING WRONG.

I SURRENDERED THE CARD AND WATCHED AS HE CUT IT INTO A DOZEN TINY PIECES.

45

A YEAR LATER, I WAS LIVING IN CHICAGO, WORKING AS A WAITRESS, AND WAS IN MY FAVORITE STORE, WONDERING HOW I COULD BUY A PAIR OF SHOES I COULDN'T AFFORD.

DO YOU HAVE A CREDIT CARD?

NO—WELL, I USED TO, BUT MY DAD CUT IT UP.

CALL THE CREDIT CARD COMPANY AND HAVE THEM SEND YOU A NEW ONE.

I WENT OUTSIDE TO CALL DISCOVER FROM A PAY PHONE.

SOCIAL SECURITY NUMBER? HOME ADDRESS? UM... DO YOU ALSO USE A P.O. BOX?

*PRE-CELL PHONE.

WHAT'S GOING ON?

THERE WAS A LONG PAUSE, INTERMITTENT TYPING.

THERE'S AN OVERDUE BALANCE OF ONE THOUSAND TWO HUNDRED AND THIRTY-SEVEN DOLLARS AND SIXTY-FIVE CENTS. LET ME TRANSFER YOU.

SHE PUT ME ON HOLD, I HEARD SOME LIGHT JAZZ, AND THEN...

COLLECTIONS.

I CALLED MY MOTHER.

WHY ARE YOU CRYING? CALM DOWN — I CAN'T HEAR YOU!

WHEN I FINALLY COMPOSED MYSELF ENOUGH TO TELL HER WHAT WAS GOING ON, SHE GREW QUIET. SHE DIDN'T ATTEMPT TO DEFEND MY FATHER OR SAY THERE HAD BEEN A MISUNDERSTANDING.

I NEED TO TALK TO DADDY.

AN HOUR LATER, SHE CALLED BACK, SOUNDING SUBDUED.

YOUR FATHER FEELS TERRIBLE, LAURIE. HE KNOWS WHAT HE DID WAS WRONG.

BUT I HAVE TO LIVE WITH THE CONSEQUENCES— MY CREDIT IS PROBABLY RUINED!

I'LL TAKE OUT A LOAN. I'LL PAY OFF THE CARD. IT WON'T AFFECT YOUR CREDIT.

LET ME SPEAK TO DAD!

MY FATHER SOUNDED EQUALLY DEFEATED.

THE DEAL I WAS WAITING FOR DIDN'T GO THROUGH. I WAS DESPERATE.

THAT'S NO EXCUSE. WHAT YOU'VE DONE IS CRIMINAL, AND WORSE—MORALLY REPREHENSIBLE. I CAN'T STAND BY AND WATCH YOU WIPE OUT MOM'S BANK ACCOUNT, OR MY FUTURE. YOU'LL BE HEARING FROM MY ATTORNEY.

ACTUALLY, THAT'S WHAT I **WISHED** I'D SAID. INSTEAD, I SIMPLY REGRESSED.

BUT I'M YOUR **DAUGHTER**. I'VE NEVER EVEN **HAD** A CREDIT CARD OF MY OWN.

MY MOTHER TOOK OUT A LOAN TO PAY OFF THE DISCOVER CARD, AND I GRADUALLY FORGAVE MY FATHER FOR WHAT I ASSUMED WAS A SINGLE TRANSGRESSION. I PROBABLY WOULDN'T HAVE FOUND OUT ABOUT THE OTHER CARDS HAD I NOT TRIED TO OPEN A BANANA REPUBLIC ACCOUNT A YEAR LATER AND GOTTEN DENIED.

CALL OUR CREDIT DEPARTMENT SO YOU CAN FIND OUT WHY YOU WERE DECLINED. MOST OF THE TIME, IT'S SOMETHING REALLY STUPID, LIKE THE INTEREST RATE ON ONE OF YOUR OTHER CREDIT CARDS WAS TOO HIGH. HERE'S THE NUMBER.

20% OFF

KATHY

I ORDERED A COPY OF THE APPLICATION MY FATHER HAD SUBMITTED TO DISCOVER.

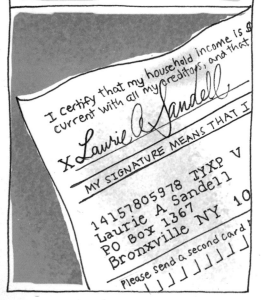

IN THE UPPER LEFT-HAND CORNER OF THE PAGE WAS A REASONABLE FACSIMILE OF MY SIGNATURE. A BIT SHAKY, PERHAPS, BUT MY SIGNATURE, NONETHELESS.

HOW DID I STAND A CHANCE AGAINST SOMEONE SO DETERMINED?

I CALLED THE SOCIAL SECURITY ADMINISTRATION TO TRY TO CHANGE MY SOCIAL SECURITY NUMBER.

IT'S POSSIBLE IF YOU FILE A FRAUD COMPLAINT AND PRESS CRIMINAL CHARGES.

I TRIED TO PICTURE MY FATHER IN AN ORANGE JUMPSUIT, SITTING ON A METAL BED, STARING AT THE FLOOR. HE WAS OVERWEIGHT. HE'D HAD THREE HEART ATTACKS AND WHEEZED WHEN HE WALKED.

I COULDN'T DO IT.

CLICK

THIS TIME, I LET MY MOTHER CONFRONT MY FATHER. AFTERWARD, SHE CALLED ME.

I'LL PAY THE OUTSTANDING BALANCES, DON'T WORRY.

TELL HIM I'VE ORDERED **CREDIT AWARE!**

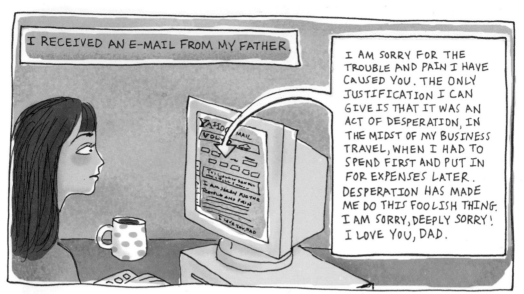

I RECEIVED AN E-MAIL FROM MY FATHER.

I AM SORRY FOR THE TROUBLE AND PAIN I HAVE CAUSED YOU. THE ONLY JUSTIFICATION I CAN GIVE IS THAT IT WAS AN ACT OF DESPERATION, IN THE MIDST OF MY BUSINESS TRAVEL, WHEN I HAD TO SPEND FIRST AND PUT IN FOR EXPENSES LATER. DESPERATION HAS MADE ME DO THIS FOOLISH THING. I AM SORRY, DEEPLY SORRY! I LOVE YOU, DAD.

YEAH, *RIGHT*!

SOON AFTER THAT, MY MOTHER CALLED TO TELL ME THE BANK HAD FORECLOSED ON MY PARENTS' HOME.

I... I GUESS HE DIDN'T MAKE SOME OF THE MORTGAGE PAYMENTS.

EVENTUALLY, TIME LESSENED THE IMPACT OF WHAT MY FATHER HAD DONE UNTIL I COULDN'T REMEMBER WHY, EXACTLY, I'D BEEN SO ANGRY AT HIM.

HE HAS **NO** MONEY. AND HE CAN'T GET A JOB BECAUSE OF HIS POLITICS.

Mm HMM.

THE NEXT FOUR YEARS WERE AN EXERCISE IN SELF-DESTRUCTION. I TRAVELED RELENTLESSLY. I TOLD MANY LIES. I WAS WILLING TO BE ANYTHING, TRY ANYTHING, AS LONG AS IT DIDN'T RESEMBLE THE LIFE I WAS LIVING BEFORE.

IN ISRAEL, I HAD MY FIRST AND ONLY LESBIAN FLING, WITH A YESHIVA GIRL NAMED SARAH.

FROM THE START, SHE WANTED TO BE MY GIRLFRIEND. I WANTED ONLY SEX.

I...I WORRY YOU'RE JUST EXPERIMENTING.

I'M **NOT**. I THINK YOU'RE REALLY SPECIAL.

THIS WENT ON FOR MONTHS: SARAH ATTEMPTING TO HOLD MY HAND IN PUBLIC, AND ME GIVING HER JUST ENOUGH AFFECTION TO LURE HER BACK TO MY APARTMENT AT THE END OF THE NIGHT.

LATER THAT NIGHT...

WHERE ARE YOU GOING?

I NEED TO WASH MY APRON FOR WORK.

BUT IT'S THREE IN THE MORNING!

YOU'RE JUST **USING ME**!

NO, I'M NOT. COME HERE.

HER EYES WERE FULL OF LONGING, REJECTION, HURT.

IT'S NOT THAT I WASN'T AWARE OF WHAT I WAS DOING TO SARAH; IT'S JUST THAT THE PART OF ME THAT WANTED TO EXPERIMENT SEXUALLY WAS SPEAKING UP MORE LOUDLY THAN THE PART OF ME THAT WANTED TO BE CARING AND COMPASSIONATE.

THERE WAS LAURIE, THE GOOD GIRL, WHO WON HER FATHER'S LOVE WITH CARTOONS AND AWARDS.

AND THERE WAS ANGRY, EMPATHY-FREE LAURIE, WHO REFUSED TO CATER TO ANYONE'S NEEDS BUT HER OWN.

ONE DAY, A WOMAN I WORKED WITH TOLD ME SHE'D JUST RETURNED FROM TOKYO, WHERE SHE'D WORKED AS A "HOSTESS," A SORT OF MODERN-DAY GEISHA. THE JOB INVOLVED MAKING CONVERSATION WITH JAPANESE BUSINESSMEN.

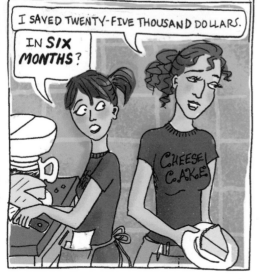

I SAVED TWENTY-FIVE THOUSAND DOLLARS.

IN *SIX* MONTHS?

TWO DAYS LATER, I SAID GOOD-BYE TO SARAH.

WHEN WERE YOU GOING TO TELL ME?

LOOK, *I* DIDN'T EVEN KNOW I WAS GOING UNTIL YESTERDAY.

I NEVER SAW SARAH—OR ANY OF THE FRIENDS I'D MADE IN ISRAEL OVER THE COURSE OF TWO YEARS—AGAIN.

WITHIN A MONTH, I WAS WORKING IN A TOKYO NIGHTCLUB CALLED THE FLAMINGO. MY NEW JOB INVOLVED FLIRTING WITH CUSTOMERS, LIGHTING THEIR CIGARETTES, AND REFILLING THEIR DRINKS. FOR THIS, I WAS PAID UPWARDS OF FOUR HUNDRED DOLLARS A NIGHT.

KONICHIWA.

THE FLAMINGO WAS ALSO A STRIP BAR. THE DANCERS, I NOTICED, MADE TRIPLE THE MONEY I MADE AND DIDN'T HAVE TO DEAL WITH CUSTOMERS.

SO KAWAII!

FIVE MONTHS INTO MY STAY IN JAPAN, I CALLED A TALENT AGENCY THAT REPRESENTED DANCERS AND SET UP AN INTERVIEW.

I TOOK A BUS TO THE OUTSKIRTS OF TOKYO. I SPENT THE RIDE NERVOUSLY REAPPLYING GLITTER TO MY EYE-LIDS AND SMOOTHING MY CRUSHED VELVET DRESS.

A JAMAICAN GUY MET ME AT THE BUS STOP AND TOOK ME TO A DINGY, EMPTY APARTMENT IN THE MIDDLE OF NOWHERE.

GIVE ME YOUR PASSPORT; I NEED TO PHOTOCOPY IT FOR YOUR APPLICATION.

I SURRENDERED MY PASSPORT.

YOU WAIT HERE.

NAIVE STOICISM IN THE FACE OF PERIL WAS SECOND NATURE TO ME.

YOU'RE LUCKY YOU'RE A GIRL! IF YOU WERE A BOY I WOULD **KILL YOU!**

WHILE I WAITED, I WATCHED A BIZARRE VIDEO CALLED SEXERCIZE. IT INVOLVED A NUDE WESTERN WOMAN LEADING A PACK OF FULLY CLOTHED JAPANESE TOURISTS AROUND A ZOO.

HERE'S YOUR PASSPORT. NOW LET'S TAKE A POLAROID SO THE CLUB OWNERS CAN GET A LOOK AT YOU.

ローリーちゃん
ストリッパー　yokohama

58

THE AGENCY PLACED ME AT A CLUB IN YOKOHAMA, ABOUT EIGHTEEN MILES FROM TOKYO.

ONCE I GOT THE HANG OF IT, I FELT POWERFUL ONSTAGE.

KONICHIWA.

PARTY PINK

THE MOVIE *STRIPTEASE* HAD JUST COME OUT IN JAPAN.

DEMI MOOORE!

DEMI MOORE!

DEMI MOOOORE!

AFTER MY SET, I WAS DIRECTED TO SIT WITH CUSTOMERS AND SOLICIT LAP DANCES.

LAP DANCE-U? TOUCH OK.

FOR THE FIRST TIME, I NOTICED WHAT WAS GOING ON IN DARKENED CORNERS AROUND THE ROOM.

I DEFLECTED THE DANGER WITH A POTENTLY UNSEXY BLEND OF CEREBRAL QUIPS, OBSCURE ALLUSIONS AND INTELLECTUAL REFERENCES.

UM, AS I WAS SAYING, I PLAY CLASSICAL PIANO AND SPEAK HEBREW. PHILIP ROTH IS ONE OF MY FAVORITE WRITERS...

NO ONE ASKED ME FOR A LAP DANCE.

YOU NOT COME BACK?

YOU DON'T UNDERSTAND— THIS ISN'T ME!

MEN

IN TRUTH, I HAD NO IDEA WHO I WAS. THIS WAS REFLECTED MOST GLARINGLY IN MY RELATIONSHIPS, WHERE I TENDED TO TAKE ON THE IDENTITY OF WHOMEVER I WAS WITH, UNTIL I BECAME ENRAGED WITH THAT ROLE AND RAN.

I WANT TO BREAK UP.

YOU...YOU WANT A HOT DOG?

IF I HELD ONTO ANY SENSE OF SELF AT ALL, IT WAS THE STORY I KEPT IN MY BACK POCKET— THE ONE I TOLD ABOUT MY FATHER. I USED IT TO BOND WITH MEN.

I'VE NEVER REALLY KNOWN WHAT HE DOES FOR A LIVING. MY FAMILY THINKS HE MIGHT BE IN THE C.I.A.

THAT'S INCREDIBLE.

YOU'RE INCREDIBLE.

DURING THAT PERIOD, THE MEN I DATED RANGED FROM THE CRUEL AND DISTANT TO THE WARM AND BORING TO EVERYTHING IN BETWEEN.

ROGUES' GALLERY

DANIEL
ARTIST

SID
PLAYWRIGHT

SCOTT
THERAPIST

OSHIK
DRUMMER

PAUL
WRITER

AYAL
FREESPIRIT

ANDY
STOCKBROKER

DAVID
DOCTOR

JEREMY
ARCHITECT

I TRAVELED MORE.

INDIA

JORDAN

MEXICO

FRANCE

EGYPT

THAILAND

I RETURNED TO AMERICA HAVING NO IDEA WHAT I'D LEARNED FROM MY TRAVELS AND NO CLUE WHAT I WAS GOING TO DO NEXT. MY SISTER, WHO'D GOTTEN A JOB IN FINANCE, SAID SHE COULD HELP ME FIND WORK AS A SECRETARY IN A BANK. MY FATHER HELPED ME WITH MY RÉSUMÉ.

BUT IF I ADD IN ALL THOSE WAITRESSING JOBS, IT'S GOING TO BE LIKE FOUR PAGES LONG!

IT **SHOULD** BE FOUR PAGES LONG. AT **LEAST**.

I GOT THE JOB. IT WASN'T EXACTLY A DREAM JOB, BUT I'D NEVER MADE MONEY LIKE THAT BEFORE.

I STILL CALLED ON MY FATHER FOR ADVICE.

I TOOK VACATION BUT PUT IN FOR OVERTIME BY MISTAKE AND GOT AN EXTRA FIVE HUNDRED DOLLARS — I'M **FREAKING OUT!**

DON'T PANIC! JUST DON'T TELL ANYONE. FOR YEARS **—YEARS—** I DIDN'T TELL THE GOVERNMENT CERTAIN THINGS, OK?

REALLY, HE WAS THE ONLY PERSON WHO UNDERSTOOD.

63

ONE NIGHT, I HAD DINNER WITH MY HIGH-SCHOOL FRIEND, JENNY, AND HER HUSBAND, ANDY, WHO WAS AN EDITOR AT A PRESTIGIOUS MEN'S MAGAZINE.

I STARTED TO TELL THEM STORIES ABOUT MY FATHER.

DID I EVER TELL YOU GUYS ABOUT THE TIME HE SMUGGLED KNIVES ON A FLIGHT OUT OF GERMANY?

YOU'VE GOTTA WRITE THIS SHIT *DOWN*. YOU COULD PUBLISH THIS.

THE NEXT TIME I SAW MY FATHER, I ASKED HIM HOW HE FELT ABOUT LETTING ME INTERVIEW HIM FOR A MAGAZINE ARTICLE

I'M SIXTY-THREE YEARS OF AGE NOW.... QUITE FRANKLY, WHAT'S GONNA HAPPEN? I NO LONGER PLAN TO RUN FOR POLITICAL OFFICE.

WHEN MY FATHER ARRIVED THE FOLLOWING WEEK, HE WAS TEN MINUTES EARLY, AS ALWAYS.

WHERE ARE THE EMTS?

64

I TOOK HIS COAT FROM HIM, A GREEN BARN JACKET DECORATED WITH A CONSTELLATION OF PINS AND MEDALS: AN AMERICAN FLAG, A PURPLE HEART, THE SKULL AND CROSSBONES OF THE SPECIAL FORCES.

HE SETTLED INTO A STIFF-BACKED CHAIR AND I SAT ACROSS FROM HIM ON THE COUCH. HE STARTED TO TALK.

TAPE RECORDER

IN NINETEEN SEVENTY-THREE, WHEN I WAS A PROFESSOR AT STANFORD, THE NIXON ADMINISTRATION OFFERED ME THE POSITION OF DEPUTY ASSISTANT SECRETARY OF STATE FOR INTER-AMERICAN AFFAIRS. SOMEHOW A SITUATION CAME ABOUT THAT I SPENT TWO AND A HALF HOURS WITH HENRY KISSINGER IN HIS OFFICE AT THE STATE DEPARTMENT. HE HAD QUITE A REPUTATION AS A LADIES' MAN BEFORE HE GOT MARRIED. WHY? **WOMEN LIKE POWER**! ANYWAY, HE WAS VERY NICE TO ME, VERY FRIENDLY, SO MUCH SO THAT SIXTEEN YEARS LATER, I BECAME A CONSULTANT TO THE NATIONAL SECURITY COUNCIL...

THAT FIRST NIGHT, HE SPOKE FOR HOURS—I JUST LISTENED. IN NO TIME, I WAS UTTERLY ENTRANCED BY MY FATHER'S STORIES.

65

HE'D RUBBED SHOULDERS WITH A FUTURE JUSTICE OF THE U.S. SUPREME COURT.

"ANTHONY KENNEDY AND I WERE COLLEAGUES AT THE UNIVERSITY OF THE PACIFIC. OH, WE USED TO TALK FOR **HOURS** IN THE FACULTY ROOM."

PARACHUTED INTO THE VIETNAMESE JUNGLE WITH GENERAL WESTMORELAND.

"THE GENERAL PLUMMETED OUT OF THE TREE, AND THAT'S HOW I BECAME KNOWN AS THE MAN WHO DROPPED WESTMORELAND!"

OH, **SHIT**!

BECOME PEN PALS WITH POPE JOHN PAUL II.

"I STARTED CORRESPONDING WITH A YOUNG POLISH MONSIGNOR WHO WAS A PROFESSOR AT THE PONTIFICAL COLLEGE IN ROME. HIS NAME WAS KAROL WOJTYLA."

IT WAS NEARING MIDNIGHT WHEN WE STOPPED.

WELL, I THINK THAT'S ENOUGH FOR TONIGHT.

"ALL OF A SUDDEN, SOMEBODY YELLS, '**GRENADE**!' IN MY PANIC— IN MY **PROFOUND** PANIC — I STOOD UP, GRABBED MY HELMET OFF, AND THAT THING CAME, AND I TURNED, AND CAUGHT IT IN THE AIR AND THREW IT BACK, WITH MY HELMET AND EVERYTHING. ALL OF A SUDDEN, '**BOOM**!' IT CAME AT ME, AND I LUNGED— I DON'T KNOW HOW; DON'T ASK ME TO REPEAT IT. IT WAS CARNAGE LIKE NOTHING ELSE."

"WHO ARE THE PROSPECTIVE BUYERS OF A TECHNOLOGY LIKE THIS ONE? PEOPLE LIKE BILL GATES, MICHAEL DELL — IN OTHER WORDS, I'M GOING TO CONTACT THE THOUSAND RICHEST MEN IN THE WORLD. BECAUSE I'VE ALREADY ESTABLISHED A LAW: I WILL NOT WORK FOR **ANYBODY** UNLESS THE MONEY IS UP FRONT. MONEY TALKS, BULLSHIT WALKS. PERIOD. AT SIXTY-THREE, IF I HAVEN'T LEARNED THAT, I'M IN REAL TROUBLE."

AND A DUEL HE'D BEEN IN, IN ARGENTINA.

"WAS MY HEART POUNDING? WHAT DO YOU MEAN, WAS IT POUNDING? IT WAS JUMPING OUT OF MY EARS! DO YOU REALIZE WHAT YOU'RE DOING HERE? YOU'RE GOING TO SHOOT AT A MAN, AND HE'S GOING TO SHOOT AT YOU, AND YOU'RE GOING TO BE DEAD!"

SOON, HE WAS DRIVING INTO THE CITY ON A WEEKLY BASIS TO MEET WITH ME. HIS STORIES, THEY WERE BECOMING AN ADDICTION.

WHO WAS THE GUY WHO HAD THE CLEANEST CLOSET? ME. WHO WAS THE GUY WHO HAD THE NEATEST LOCKER? ME. WHO WAS THE GUY WHO HAD THE BEST-PRESSED CLOTHES AND THE SMARTEST SALUTE? ME. AND DON'T THINK FOR A MOMENT THAT THE COMPANY COMMANDER DIDN'T NOTICE.

DURING THESE CONVERSATIONS, I IGNORED THE PHONE. I DIDN'T HEAR MY ROOMMATE COME IN. I FELT CLOSER TO MY FATHER THAN I HAD IN YEARS.

DID I BELIEVE HIM? HALF OF ME DID.

THE OTHER HALF **WANTED** TO BELIEVE HIM BUT HAD SERIOUS RESERVATIONS.

I SPENT ALL DAY, EVERY DAY, AT MY SECRETARIAL JOB, TRANSCRIBING INTERVIEWS.

AT NIGHT, I WOULD LIE IN BED, READING AND REREADING THE TRANSCRIPTS.

STAYING UP LATE TO READ TRANSCRIPTS, THEN GETTING UP EARLY FOR WORK TOOK ITS TOLL— I STARTED TO HAVE TERRIBLE INSOMNIA.

I MENTIONED THE TROUBLE I WAS HAVING TO MY MOTHER—I KNEW SHE SUFFERED FROM INSOMNIA TOO.

HAVE YOU EVER TRIED AMBIEN?

SHE SENT ME A HANDFUL OF PILLS AND TOLD ME TO BREAK THEM IN HALF.

I WAITED UNTIL SUNDAY TO TAKE ONE—THE NIGHT I TENDED TO HAVE THE MOST TROUBLE FALLING ASLEEP.

69

WITHIN MINUTES, I WAS OUT COLD, IN THE KIND OF DEEP, DREAMY SLUMBER I HADN'T EXPERIENCED SINCE CHILDHOOD.

THE NEXT MORNING I WOKE UP REFRESHED. WITHIN THREE WEEKS, I WAS TAKING IT EVERY NIGHT, MY SLEEP TROUBLES OVER.

EVERY SO OFTEN, ANDY, WHO WAS NOW MY EDITOR, WOULD CHECK IN, AND I'D TELL HIM THE LATEST STORY.

HE TOLD YOU WHAT? YOU DON'T BELIEVE HIM, DO YOU? THOSE STORIES ARE INSANE!

THE TALES HE TOLD **WERE** INSANE AND YET...

"OUR SECOND-IN-COMMANDS CHECKED OUR PISTOLS TO MAKE SURE THAT THEY WERE LOADED, AND WE STOOD BACK-TO-BACK."

READING THE TRANSCRIPTS IN ORDER, ABSORBING THE STORIES AS A WHOLE...

"THERE WAS ONE THING THEY DIDN'T COUNT ON: THIS YOUNG KID, THIS YOUNG PUP THAT THEY WERE DEFYING, WAS A CRACK SHOT. THEY DIDN'T KNOW THAT. **I** KNEW THAT."

I SECRETLY BELIEVED THERE WAS A POSSIBILITY HE WAS TELLING THE TRUTH.

"THEN THEY SAY, '**FUEGO**!' FIRE! HIS BULLET PASSED ME LIKE THIS. I'M NOT KIDDING YOU, SWEETIE. I **FELT** IT. NO QUESTION. MINE, UNFORTUNATELY, LANDED RIGHT HERE, BETWEEN THE EYES. I KILLED HIM. BELIEVE ME, A BULLET GOES RIGHT THROUGH."

AFTER ALL, I'D **SEEN** MY FATHER PERFORM ASTOUNDING FEATS WITH MY OWN EYES.

WANT TO TRY IT?

OF COURSE, I WAS A CHILD THEN, AND NOT TRAINED TO LOOK FOR INCONSISTENCIES.

THE LIEUTENANT COMMANDER SAID, "TAKE YOUR BERET OFF." THEN HE HANDED ME A GREEN BERET WITH THE SPECIAL FORCES LOGO ON IT. I LOOKED AT IT, TOTALLY SHOCKED, AND SAID, 'BUT I DIDN'T GO THROUGH TRAINING...' HE SAID, 'DON'T YOU WORRY, SON. IF YOU SURVIVE THE NEXT SIX MONTHS HERE, YOU WILL HAVE EARNED IT.'

THE INTERVIEWS CONTINUED. EVENTUALLY, I HAD MORE THAN THREE HUNDRED PAGES TRANSCRIBED. ANDY KEPT CALLING TO SEE IF I'D FACT-CHECKED MY FATHER'S CLAIMS.

WHAT ARE YOU WAITING FOR? CALL THE UNIVERSITIES.

HE STILL HASN'T TOLD ME ABOUT LANGUAGE SCHOOL, AND I DON'T WANT TO INTERRUPT OUR GROOVE.

REALLY, I JUST DIDN'T **WANT** TO KNOW. THE STORIES KEPT OUR RELATIONSHIP INTACT. TO BE HONEST, THEY WERE KEEPING **ME** INTACT.

ONE DAY, I OPENED UP MY OLD HOTMAIL ACCOUNT, WHICH I HADN'T USED IN AGES, AND FOUND AN E-MAIL FROM MY FATHER. IT WAS JUST A FEW DAYS OLD.

ONE QUICK GLANCE AND I KNEW IT WASN'T INTENDED FOR ME. IT SEEMED HE HAD CC'D ME BY MISTAKE.

TO: MAIFENG@HOTMAIL.COM
MY BELOVED MAI,
AFTER OUR CONVERSATION LAST NIGHT, I FELT TERRIBLY SAD. AFTER SIXTY-THREE YEARS OF SUCCESS, HAVING BECOME FAMOUS, HAVING ACCOMPLISHED EVERYTHING I HAD SET OUT TO DO, I FIND MYSELF NOW TO BE A LOSER, AND AM NOT SURE I CAN HANDLE ALL THESE REVERSES AT THE SAME TIME. THE FEELING THAT YOU WERE WITH ME IS THE ONLY THING THAT HAS SUSTAINED ME ALL THESE MONTHS. REGARDLESS OF THE SITUATION, I WILL HELP YOU ANYWAY. UNFORTUNATELY, I DON'T HAVE THE WEALTH THAT I ONCE HAD, OTHERWISE I WOULD HELP YOU A LOT MORE. I LOVE YOU AND ALWAYS WILL.

I CALLED KARYN.

ARE YOU KIDDING? READ IT TO ME AGAIN.

CLEARLY, HE HAD NO IDEA HE'D SENT ME THIS E-MAIL — NOR WAS HE IN THE MIDDLE OF KILLING HIMSELF.

THESE PAST TWO YEARS, WE'D GROWN AS CLOSE AS I'D EVER IMAGINED WE COULD POSSIBLY BE. I'D BEEN SUCKED INTO TRUSTING HIM **AGAIN**. I WAS ANGRIER AT MYSELF THAN I WAS AT HIM.

AS SOON AS I HUNG UP, I MADE THREE CALLS: TO COLUMBIA UNIVERSITY, WHERE MY FATHER GOT HIS PHD; TO NYU, WHERE HE GOT HIS JD, AND TO STANFORD UNIVERSITY, WHERE HE TAUGHT ECONOMICS.

NONE OF THEM HAD EVER HEARD OF HIM.

I CALLED THE COMMUNITY COLLEGE WHERE MY FATHER HAD WORKED FROM 1981 TO 1983. I MANAGED TO TRACK DOWN THE DEAN WHO HAD HIRED HIM.

I REMEMBER YOUR FATHER WELL—HE WAS ONE OF THE BEST TEACHERS WE EVER HAD. BUT THEN HE CHANGED. HE BECAME AGGRESSIVE WITH COLLEAGUES, ALMOST BIPOLAR.

AT THE END OF THE SEMESTER, HE TURNED IN A STACK OF STUDENT EVALUATIONS, EVERY SINGLE ONE OF THEM MARKED "EXCELLENT"— ALL IN THE SAME PEN, SAME HANDWRITING.

I DID MY OWN BACKGROUND CHECK AND FOUND OUT THAT HE'D BEEN IMPERSONATING A HARVARD PROFESSOR. WHEN I CONFRONTED HIM, HE HANDED IN HIS RESIGNATION AND LEFT WITHOUT SAYING GOOD-BYE. I HEARD HE WAS TEACHING AT RAMAPO COLLEGE AFTER THAT.

DID YOU WARN THE ADMINISTRATION THERE?

NO. I LIKED YOUR FATHER VERY MUCH.

I SENT AWAY FOR MY FATHER'S MILITARY RECORDS AND RECEIVED A TWO-PAGE DOCUMENT FROM THE NATIONAL PERSONNEL RECORDS CENTER. HIS RANK WAS LISTED AS PRIVATE. NO PURPLE HEARTS OR BRONZE STARS. NO MENTION OF HIS EVER HAVING SET FOOT IN VIETNAM.

I CALLED MY MOTHER TO SEE WHAT SHE HAD TO SAY. TO MY SURPRISE, SHE DIDN'T EXACTLY DENY THE CHARGES.

BUT HE **TOLD** ME HE HAD THOSE DEGREES.

WHAT DO YOU MEAN, HE 'TOLD' YOU? DID YOU SEE HIM STUDYING? MEET HIS GRAD SCHOOL BUDDIES?

STOP BOMBARDING ME WITH QUESTIONS— I CAN HARDLY THINK.

AN HOUR LATER, MY PHONE RANG AGAIN. IT WAS MY MOTHER, SPEAKING IN A VOICE THAT SOUNDED ALMOST ROBOTIC.

THERE ARE REASONS, SOMETIMES, WHY PEOPLE'S NAMES AREN'T IN THE PUBLIC EYE.

WHAT? IS DAD TELLING YOU TO SAY THAT?

I HAVE TO GO.

I RECOGNIZED MY MOTHER'S BLIND FAITH IN MY FATHER.

DIAL TONE

IT LOOKED LIKE THE FAITH **I** ONCE HAD.

THIS EXQUISITE SET OF ROSARY BEADS WAS GIVEN TO MY FATHER BY THE POPE HIMSELF.

IN THAT MOMENT, ANY RESERVATIONS I HAD ABOUT WRITING ABOUT MY FATHER EVAPORATED. I CALLED UP MY SISTERS AND MY EDITOR, ANDY, TO TELL THEM WHAT I PLANNED TO DO.

YOU'RE GOING TO **PUBLISH** THIS?

BUT WHAT ABOUT MOM?

ARE YOU SURE YOU'RE READY TO DO THIS? EXPOSE YOUR FATHER AS A FRAUD IN FRONT OF THE WHOLE WORLD?

RELATIVE IMPOSTOR

ONE WEEK LATER, I ASKED MY FATHER TO MEET ME AT STARBUCKS.

SO, I DON'T KNOW HOW MUCH MOM TOLD YOU—

IF YOU EVER HAVE SOMETHING TO TELL ME, THE **LAST** PERSON I WANT YOU TO TALK TO IS MY WIFE.

SLAM.

WHAT'S THAT FOR?

I'M OLD, HIJA, WHAT CAN I TELL YOU?

DAD, I CHECKED WITH SOME OF THE UNIVERSITIES YOU SAY YOU WENT TO, AND, UM, THEY'VE NEVER HEARD OF YOU.

YOU ARE WALKING INTO A MINEFIELD.

I DON'T CARE IF YOU'VE KILLED PEOPLE. I DON'T CARE IF YOU'RE RUNNING A BABY-SMUGGLING RING. YOU CAN TELL ME.

THAT'S GOOD TO KNOW. BUT IT'S TOO LATE. I'M IN TOO DEEP.

FATHER FICTION

I LEFT THE BANK TO BECOME A FREELANCE WRITER. MY FATHER AND I DIDN'T SPEAK WHILE I WORKED ON THE STORY.

YOU KNOW, DADDY CAME INTO THE CITY SO MANY TIMES TO TALK TO YOU.

I KNOW.

WELL, HE'S NOT GOING TO TALK TO YOU ANYMORE. I'M NOT SURE HE'S *EVER* GOING TO TALK TO YOU AGAIN.

I KNOW.

AND WHAT AM I SUPPOSED TO TELL PEOPLE—THAT YOU'RE WRITING A TELL-ALL ABOUT US?

TELL THEM WHATEVER YOU WANT.

THE TEACHERS AT SCHOOL TALK. MY COUSINS TALK.

I CAN'T WORRY ABOUT WHAT PEOPLE SAY ANYMORE.

83

MY BIRTHDAY WENT BY WITHOUT A PHONE CALL FROM MY FATHER, SO I KNEW HE MEANT BUSINESS. MOTHER'S DAY, FATHER'S DAY, AND MY MOTHER'S BIRTHDAY ALL PASSED. MY PARENTS AND SISTERS MET UP FOR HOLIDAYS WITHOUT ME.

MY SISTERS WERE SUPPORTIVE OF ME, BUT NOT OF THE STORY I WAS WRITING.

OK, SO HE WASN'T IN VIETNAM. BUT DO YOU HAVE TO PUBLICLY HUMILIATE HIM?

CAN'T YOU JUST SEE A SHRINK?

FREEDOM OF INFORMATION ACT

I DID FEEL GUILTY. HADN'T HE WRITTEN A BAY OF PIGS PAPER FOR ME IN THE SEVENTH GRADE? AND THIS WAS HOW I REPAID HIM...

OTHER TIMES, ANGER ECLIPSED MY GUILT. HE'D LIED TO ME AS A KID! AS A TEEN! AS A *JOURNALIST*!

FOR THE MOMENT, I IGNORED MY DILEMMA AND SPENT ALL MY TIME WRITING AT THE NEW YORK PUBLIC LIBRARY. SEEING MY FATHER'S CRIMES LAID OUT ON-SCREEN DIDN'T MAKE THE ACT OF EXPOSING HIM EASIER; IF ANYTHING, *I* FELT EXPOSED. I WAS THE MONSTER MY FATHER HAD ALWAYS ACCUSED ME OF BEING, THE BAD SEED. IF MY FATHER DIED OF A HEART ATTACK AFTER HE READ IT, I'D BE RESPONSIBLE. IT WAS AN UNDERLYING FEAR I'D HAD SINCE I WAS TWELVE YEARS OLD — SOMEHOW, IN SOME WAY, I'D BE RESPONSIBLE FOR HIS DEMISE. AND YET...

I KNEW I WASN'T GOING TO BE FREE OF HIM UNTIL I UNDERSTOOD HIM. HE'D IMPLICATED ME IN HIS CRIMES, MAKING THEM MY CRIMES. HIS STORY WAS MY STORY TOO.

A PRIVATE INVESTIGATOR?! AM I IN SOME KIND OF TROUBLE?

THE MAN'S NAME WAS AL MCEVOY. HE WAS REPRESENTING A MAN NAMED JORGE LOPEZ.

IN SEPTEMBER, YOUR FATHER WENT TO CHINA TO SELL SOME TECHNOLOGY ON MY CLIENT'S BEHALF. HE HASN'T HEARD FROM HIM SINCE. IS YOUR FATHER STILL IN THE COUNTRY?

I HAVE NO IDEA. WE'RE NOT... IN TOUCH.

WOULD YOU BE WILLING TO TALK TO MR. LOPEZ? SAYS HE'S A FRIEND. HE JUST WANTS TO MAKE SURE YOUR FATHER IS OK.

DO YOU WANT TO GIVE ME HIS NUMBER?

ACTUALLY, HE'LL CALL YOU, AT NOON. HE'S IN A HOTEL IN MANHATTAN.

12:00 P.M. SHARP

CLICK

FIRST, I MUST APOLOGIZE: I AM TERRIBLY SORRY TO DISTURB YOU. IT'S JUST THAT MY WIFE AND I HAVE NOT HEARD FROM YOUR FATHER AND ARE WORRIED ABOUT HIM.

SO YOU'RE A FRIEND OF HIS?

A FRIEND AND BUSINESS PARTNER. ABOUT A YEAR AGO, MY WIFE AND I SENT HIM ON A TRIP TO CHINA TO SELL SOME TECHNOLOGY WE'D INVENTED...

HE WAS GOING TO SELL IT TO THE WORLD'S THOUSAND RICHEST MEN?

YES, THAT'S IT! AND WE HAVEN'T HEARD FROM HIM SINCE. I'VE SENT LETTERS, MANY E-MAILS, AND LEFT PHONE MESSAGES. BUT HE HASN'T RESPONDED TO ANY OF THEM.

WHO IS THIS PRIVATE INVESTIGATOR WHO CALLED ME?

WELL, WHEN I VISITED THE POLICE STATION IN BRONXVILLE...

THE **POLICE**?

YES, WHEN YOUR FATHER DIDN'T RESPOND TO ANY OF MY LETTERS I FLEW TO NEW YORK TO CHECK ON MY INVESTMENT.

AND WHAT IS IT YOU WANT FROM MY FATHER?

I WOULD LIKE TO RECEIVE THE MATERIALS HE HAS PROMISED TO DELIVER AND RECEIPTS FOR THE MONEY WE'VE SENT.

HOW MUCH HAVE YOU PAID HIM ALREADY?

I SEE. SO A TOTAL OF THREE HUNDRED AND FORTY THOUSAND DOLLARS.

I TOOK HIS INFORMATION AND GOT OFF THE PHONE. MY HEART HURT FOR THIS MAN. I KNEW HE WOULD NEVER SEE HIS MONEY AGAIN.

MY ARTICLE ON MY FATHER APPEARED IN APRIL. I DIDN'T PUT MY NAME ON IT.

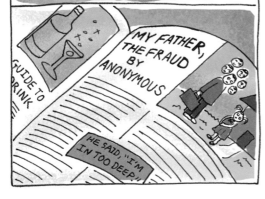

GUIDE TO DRINK

MY FATHER, THE FRAUD BY ANONYMOUS

HE SAID, "I'M IN TOO DEEP."

EACH OF MY FAMILY MEMBERS REACTED TO IT IN THEIR OWN WAY.

OH, **THAT**— WELL, I'M NOT PLANNING TO READ IT.

SO IS IT OUT OF YOUR SYSTEM NOW?

BARNEY'S

WHY DIDN'T YOU TELL ME ABOUT THE LETTER? I WANT TO KNOW MORE... WAIT, DON'T TELL ME. I FEEL TOO GUILTY.

DID MY FATHER READ THE STORY? TO THIS DAY, I DON'T KNOW. BY THE TIME IT CAME OUT, WE HADN'T SPOKEN IN MORE THAN A YEAR. AS FOR ME, I THOUGHT IT WOULD PROVIDE THE KIND OF CATHARSIS I'D BEEN LOOKING FOR, BUT I FELT MORE UNMOORED THAN EVER. NOTHING HAD CHANGED: MY FAMILY CONTINUED TO BE INSISTENTLY BLIND TO THE TRUTH. I REMAINED THE LONE VOICE OF PROTEST. THE PIECE SAT ANONYMOUSLY ON NEWSSTANDS, THEN JUST AS QUIETLY DISAPPEARED.

STAR STRUCK

SOON AFTER, I LANDED A JOB AT A POPULAR WOMEN'S MAGAZINE.

MY MOTHER BRAGGED ABOUT MY NEW JOB TO ALL HER FRIENDS. MAINLY, SHE WAS RELIEVED I'D WRITTEN THE STORY ABOUT MY DAD ANONYMOUSLY.

EVERYONE WAS SO IMPRESSED WHEN THEY HEARD YOU'RE GOING TO BE ON STAFF!

ONE DAY, MY EDITOR WAS IN A PANIC. THE WRITER FOR OUR SEPTEMBER COVER STORY ON PENÉLOPE CRUZ HAD FALLEN THROUGH. SHE ASKED IF I WOULD LIKE TO DO A LAST-MINUTE INTERVIEW WITH THE SPANISH STAR.

WHAT DO YOU THINK?

WOULD I **LIKE** TO? I WAS **_THRILLED_**!

CELEBRITY TRIVIA WAS A SECRET HOBBY OF MINE. I READ TABLOIDS BY THE BUSHEL. I ACTUALLY KNEW PENELOPE WAS VACATIONING WITH MATTHEW MCCONAUGHEY AT A RESORT SOMEWHERE IN LOUISIANA.

HERE'S WHERE THEY'RE STAYING.

MAPQUEST

THE INTERVIEW WENT OFF WITHOUT A HITCH.

THIS EES PENÉLOPE.

THANK YOU—THAT EES VERY SWEET!

OH, TOM* AND I ARE STILL GREAT FRIENDS.

*CRUISE

EM, I WOULD SAY PEDRO ALMODÓVAR.

I AM MORE PROUD OF THEES FILM THAN ANY OTHER.

CIAO!

NEXT THING I KNEW, I WAS FLYING TO LOS ANGELES TO INTERVIEW CARMEN ELECTRA.

HERE'S WHY THIS IS AN IMPORTANT ASSIGNMENT. SHE'S GOING TO TALK ABOUT THE DEATHS OF HER MOTHER AND SISTER.

AND STAYING AT THE FOUR SEASONS IN BEVERLY HILLS.

FOUR SEASONS

I'D FORGOTTEN HOW MUCH I HATED TO FLY.

THE LONG HAUL

THEN I REMEMBERED THE AMBIEN IN MY BAG. I'D BEEN TAKING IT EVERY NIGHT TO SLEEP — WHY NOT TO FLY?

I POPPED A PILL. FIFTEEN MINUTES LATER, MY FEAR HAD MELTED AWAY ENTIRELY. I WOKE UP WHEN WE TOUCHED DOWN ON THE TARMAC.

MISS, WE'RE HERE.

I WAS STILL GROGGY WHEN I CHECKED IN, SO I TOOK A LONG, LUXURIOUS NAP IN MY KING-SIZE BED. I WOKE UP REFRESHED AND **THRILLED** WITH MY SURROUNDINGS.

THAT NIGHT, I HAD DINNER WITH A GIRLFRIEND OF MINE WHO LIVED IN L.A.

WHEN YOU DROP ME OFF, CAN YOU SHOW ME HOW TO USE THAT NERVE-DOT-COM SERVICE?

I'M TELLING YOU, IT'S THE GREATEST. LIKE SHOPPING THROUGH AN ONLINE CATALOGUE OF MEN.

I'D GOTTEN A FEW BOYFRIENDS OUT OF THE INTERNET DATING THING AND THOUGHT SHE OUGHT TO TRY IT. THAT'S WHEN I STUMBLED ACROSS BEN'S PROFILE.

OOH, HE'S CUTE—MIND IF I TAKE THIS ONE FOR MYSELF?

BEN WAS A SCREENWRITER WHO HAD GREAT TASTE IN BOOKS.

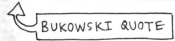

BEN 310   SILVER

"I'M A GENIUS AND NOBODY KNOWS IT BUT ME."

BUKOWSKI QUOTE

ADD TO FAVORITE PHOTOS

BEN310 has 1 photo
Upgrade to see full-size photos

Interact with BEN310
☑ Send an email   ☺ Flirt
⊘ Block emails/winks   ⇨ Refer to a friend
▤ Add to Hotlist   ⚇ Invite to Network

31-year-old Man in Los Angeles, CA

Me

Height: 6 ft. 1 in
Body Type: Athletic
Hair Color: Brown
Eye Color: Blue
Last visit: Today
Occupation: Screenwriter
Education: College
Ethnicity: Caucasian
Speaks: English
Religion: Agnostic
Cigarettes: I'm a nonsmoker
Booze: I'm a light/social drinker
Drugs: I don't use drugs

THE PHOTO HE'D POSTED WAS A SIMPLE ONE, A SELF-PORTRAIT IN FRONT OF A WHITE WALL.

BEN310 has 1 photo
Upgrade to see full-size photos

HIS PROFILE STOOD OUT BECAUSE HE SEEMED SO HUMBLE. HIS WRITING WAS CLEAR AND STRAIGHTFORWARD—THE PERSON I IMAGINED *HE* WAS.

HERE GOES NOTHING.

CLICK!

THE NEXT DAY, I HEADED OVER TO THE BEVERLY HILLS HOTEL TO INTERVIEW CARMEN ELECTRA.

MADAME, THIS WAS MARILYN MONROE'S FAVORITE BUNGALOW. WOULD YOU LIKE ME TO LIGHT A FIRE?

I'D BEEN ALLOWED TO RENT IT FOR A FEW HOURS SO WE COULD HAVE A PRIVATE CONVERSATION. IT WAS SO **BEAUTIFUL.**

IT WAS STRANGE, ALMOST IRONIC TO HAVE BEEN USHERED INTO A PLACE LIKE THIS. MY FATHER HAD WHEEDLED AND SCHEMED TO ACHIEVE FAR LESS.

RIGHT OVER HERE IS FINE.

TWENTY MINUTES LATER, MY CELL PHONE RANG.

CARMEN HURT HER FOOT DANCING WITH THE PUSSYCAT DOLLS. CAN YOU COME TO HER HOUSE INSTEAD?

I RAN TO THE FRONT DESK TO SEE IF I COULD CANCEL THE ROOM.

SORRY, THERE'S NOTHING WE CAN DO. WE'LL HAVE TO CHARGE YOU FOR THE BREAKFAST TOO.

OK, CAN YOU PUT IT ON MY CORPORATE CARD?

RUMMAGE RUMMAGE

WHEN I ENTERED THE HOUSE, I FOUND IT VIRTUALLY UNFURNISHED SAVE FOR A WHITE COUCH, A BLACK GRAND PIANO, AND AN AIRBRUSHED PAINTING OF CARMEN ELECTRA'S FACE THAT TOOK UP AN ENTIRE WALL.

WE SETTLED IN ON THE COUCH. AS SOON AS I STARTED TO ASK QUESTIONS, MY NERVOUSNESS WENT AWAY. FIGURING OUT WHAT A PERSON WANTED TO TALK ABOUT, BECOMING ABSORBED IN THEIR STORIES — THAT WAS MY SPECIALTY.

WHEN YOU ARRIVED AT YOUR SISTER'S HOUSE, WHAT DID YOU SEE?

THE TREES... THE HOUSE... EVERYTHING THAT WAS BEAUTIFUL WAS DEAD.

TAPE RECORDER

I FLEW BACK TO NEW YORK, WROTE THE STORY, AND WAS TOLD IT HAD MOVED MY EDITOR TO TEARS.

AMERICAN

IT LOOKED, AT LAST, LIKE I'D FOUND MY CALLING.

STARS!

I HAD A GIFT FOR CONNECTING WITH CELEBRITIES.

"CARMEN, I KNOW EXACTLY WHAT YOU'RE TALKING ABOUT."
"YOU DO?"
"I DO."

AND I DID.

MOST OF THEM LIVED IN EMOTIONAL CASTLES SURROUNDED BY MOATS, AND I'D BEEN BUILDING A TOWER AROUND MYSELF FOR THIRTY-TWO YEARS.

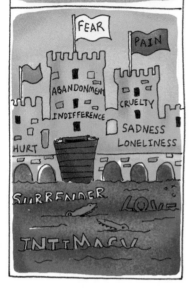

LIKE THE WOMEN I INTERVIEWED, I'D PERFECTED THE ART OF SEEMING INCREDIBLY OPEN, WITHOUT GIVING TOO MUCH OF MYSELF AWAY.

AND I KNEW JUST HOW TO VALIDATE WHATEVER IDENTITY THEY WANTED TO CREATE.

IT WAS A SKILL THAT COULDN'T BE FAKED— ONE I'D BEEN CULTIVATING ALL MY LIFE.

TWO DAYS AFTER MY INTERVIEW, I RETURNED TO NEW YORK. THERE WAS AN E-MAIL WAITING FOR ME FROM BEN.

HI LAURIE,
YOU SOUND SO INTERESTING. TOO BAD YOU LIVE IN BROOKLYN. I WAS INTRIGUED BY YOUR BOOK CHOICES BECAUSE I'VE READ AND ENJOYED ALL BUT MAYBE ONE OR TWO OF THEM. *THIS BOY'S LIFE* IS ONE OF MY FAVORITES. I KNOW WE LIVE QUITE FAR APART, BUT I WOULD LOVE TO KNOW MORE ABOUT YOU. AND OK, IF YOU'D LIKE TO SHARE ANY JUICY DETAILS ABOUT YOUR CARMEN ELECTRA INTERVIEW, I WOULDN'T THINK LESS OF YOU.   —BEN

I RESPONDED RIGHT AWAY. SOON, WE WERE EXCHANGING DAILY MISSIVES.

WOW, YOU'RE TURNING ME ON WITH ALL THIS BOOK TALK. I AM A GIGANTIC PHILIP ROTH FAN. I'VE PROBABLY READ MORE OF HIM THAN ANY OTHER AUTHOR.

EVERY AFTERNOON I RAN HOME TO SEE IF HE'D WRITTEN.

I'M JUST HAPPY THAT BASEBALL SEASON IS GOING TO START SOON. I LOVE FOLLOWING THE BOX SCORES.

HE TOLD ME ABOUT HIS SISTER, WHO'D BEEN KILLED IN A CAR CRASH.

WOW ABOUT YOUR SISTER. ARE YOU FINDING IT DIFFICULT TO MAKE THE FILM ABOUT HER?

THE WHOLE STORY ABOUT YOUR FATHER IS JUST FASCINATING. YOU COULD SELL THE MOVIE RIGHTS TOMORROW IF YOU WANTED.

WE WERE BOTH ATTEMPTING TO MAKE ART OUT OF THE TRAGEDIES OF OUR FAMILY LIVES.

MY FATHER KNEW VERY WELL THAT I WAS WRITING THE STORY ABOUT HIM, BUT I THINK HE WAS IN SOME KIND OF DENIAL. I THINK HE FELT THAT BY TELLING HIS STORY TO A MAGAZINE IT WOULD BECOME REAL; IT WOULD BE LEGITIMIZED. AND I WAS IN MY OWN KIND OF DENIAL, BECAUSE I DIDN'T WANT TO DEBUNK THE MYTH AND POSSIBLY DESTROY OUR RELATIONSHIP.

MY HOURS AT WORK GREW LONGER. NIGHT AFTER NIGHT, I STAYED AT THE OFFICE, SOMETIMES UNTIL MIDNIGHT OR LATER, WORKING ON MY CELEBRITY INTERVIEWS.

YOU'RE STILL HERE?

WHAT WAS THERE TO RUSH HOME TO? I'D MOVED TO MY OWN APARTMENT IN BROOKLYN, BUT I HAD NO HUSBAND OR KIDS, NO PETS, NOT EVEN A PLANT.

I *DID* HAVE BEN, BUT BEN WAS PORTABLE.

I DON'T OFTEN GET LONELY. I THINK THE MOST LONELY I'VE EVER FELT WAS WHEN I WAS IN A RELATIONSHIP THAT WASN'T WORKING.

EVENTUALLY, I WAS SENT OUT TO L.A. AGAIN.

UNLESS HE'S QUASIMODO, I'M SLEEPING WITH HIM.

GENEVIEVE FIELD

BEN AND I SPOKE ON THE PHONE FOR THE FIRST TIME THE NIGHT BEFORE I FLEW TO L.A. I SWALLOWED MY NERVOUSNESS AND PRETENDED I WAS THE MOST CONFIDENT PERSON IN THE WORLD. HE WAS JUST AS ENGAGING ON THE PHONE AS HE WAS IN HIS E-MAILS.

SO I PLANNED ACCORDINGLY.

SEXY THONGS

CONDOMS

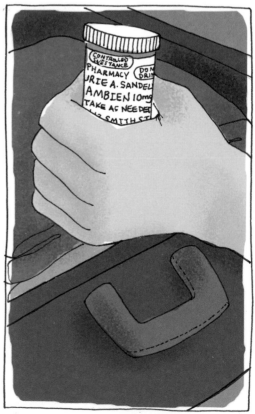

CONTROLLED SUBSTANCE
PHARMACY
...RIE A. SANDEL...
AMBIEN 10mg
TAKE AS NEEDED
...2 SMITH ST...

THE NIGHT I ARRIVED, WE MET AT THE BAR IN THE FOUR SEASONS HOTEL. WHEN WE FINALLY SAW EACH OTHER, I HAD TO READJUST MY MENTAL IMAGE OF HIM. HE WAS TALL AND HANDSOME BUT **SO** NOT MY TYPE. I LIKED SCRUFFY ARTIST-TYPE GUYS. HE WAS CLEAN-CUT, WITH A SQUARE JAW AND A CLEFT CHIN — AN EVEN MANLIER GEORGE CLOONEY.

HE WAS ALMOST **TOO** HANDSOME, IN A WAY THAT HAD ME WONDERING IF HE'D EVER BEEN SCREAMED AT IN THE BASEMENT BY HIS FATHER, HAD HIS ARM GRABBED AND SQUEEZED LIKE SOMEONE WAS TAKING HIS BLOOD PRESSURE, OR BEEN THE TARGET OF A SPEEDING BOTTLE OF TAB.

SO, DO YOU LIKE L.A.?

I DO. IT CAN BE A STRANGE PLACE, THOUGH.

WELL, I'M PRETTY ATTACHED TO NEW YORK. THERE'S SOMETHING ABOUT THE CITY THAT FEELS GRITTY BUT REAL, LIKE MY FAVORITE LINE FROM THAT LEONARD COHEN SONG, "CHELSEA HOTEL." "WE ARE UGLY, BUT WE HAVE THE MUSIC."

I GET IT. I LOVE NEW YORK. WHENEVER I VISIT, THERE IS A PART OF ME THAT FEELS REALLY AT HOME.

LATER, I INVITED HIM UP TO MY ROOM. WE LAY ON THE BED, FACING EACH OTHER, TALKING FOR HOURS. HE STILL DIDN'T MAKE A MOVE.

I'VE ALWAYS WONDERED WHAT THE ROOMS LOOKED LIKE HERE.

THESE BEDS ARE COMFY, AREN'T THEY?

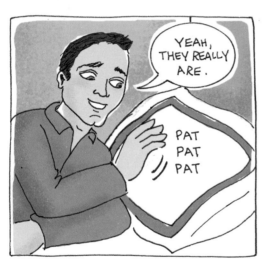

YEAH, THEY REALLY ARE.

PAT PAT PAT

FINALLY

DO YOU JUST WANT TO BE FRIENDS?

NO.

WHAT'S WRONG?

FROM THE MINUTE I MET HIM, I HAD A SUBTLE SENSE THAT *I* HAD THE UPPER HAND. REAL OR IMAGINED, IT DIDN'T MATTER: THAT FEELING OF CONTROL ALLOWED ME TO LET DOWN MY GUARD.

YOU'VE GOT A GREAT ASS.

THANK YOU.

LOVE, LUST, INFATUATION — THEY HAD ALWAYS BEEN TOO SCARY FOR ME. WHENEVER THOSE FEELINGS CROPPED UP, I LOST MYSELF INSTANTLY.

DID I... DID I WAKE YOU?

HUH?

TAP TAP

Maise

THE ANTIDOTE, I'D FOUND, WAS TO ENSURE I NEVER FELT VULNERABLE. I DID THAT BY DATING MEN WHO LIKED ME MORE THAN I LIKED THEM.

I HAVE TO GO BUT I DON'T WANT TO.

I'LL KEEP YOUR SIDE OF THE BED WARM.

WHEN I RETURNED TO NEW YORK, I SENT BEN A LIGHT, JOKEY E-MAIL.

IF I WAS DRIVING A RENTAL CAR FROM THE FOUR SEASONS TO THE L'ERMITAGE HOTEL AND THE WIND VELOCITY WAS 65 MPH, HOW LONG WOULD IT TAKE ME TO GET THERE IF I DIDN'T KNOW HOW TO TURN ON THE RENTAL CAR'S HEAD-LIGHTS, LET ALONE DRIVE FROM POINT A TO POINT B?

BUT SOMEHOW, IT WASN'T THE SAME. BEN WANTED MORE.

I'M BACK FROM SAN DIEGO ON SUNDAY. MAYBE I'LL GIVE YOU A CALL. I FEEL LIKE OUR RELATIONSHIP CAN HANDLE THE OCCASIONAL PHONE CALL NOW, RIGHT?

MEANWHILE, AT WORK, I SCORED MY NEXT BIG ASSIGNMENT. IT WAS OUR OCTOBER COVER STORY, AN IN-PERSON INTERVIEW WITH ASHLEY JUDD. THE INTERVIEW WAS SCHEDULED FOR TWO DAYS FROM THEN.

RESEARCH

BEN HAD DECIDED TO VISIT ME IN NEW YORK, AND IT WAS TOO LATE TO CHANGE HIS TICKET. THE DAY HE ARRIVED, I GOT ON A PLANE. WE DIDN'T EVEN GET TO SAY HELLO TO ONE ANOTHER.

THE INTERVIEW TOOK PLACE IN DETROIT, WHERE JUDD'S HUSBAND, A RACECAR DRIVER, WAS PARTICIPATING IN A QUALIFYING RACE.

MICHIGAN INTERNATIONAL SPEEDWAY

THAT WAY.

I OPENED THE DOOR TO HER TRAILER TO FIND HER SITTING AT A TINY LITTLE TABLE. SHE WAS **BEAUTIFUL** AND TRULY LOOKED LIKE A MOVIE STAR: SHE WORE A TANGLE OF DIAMOND NECKLACES, AND HER HAIR WAS ARTFULLY TOUSLED.

NERVOUS WRECK

BUTTERMILK, *NO*!

I TRIED TO ACT NATURAL WHILE SHE FINISHED UP WORK ON HER COMPUTER.

NOWHERE TO PUT LEFT HAND.

WHEN THE INTERVIEW BEGAN, I WAS IMMEDIATELY IN OVER MY HEAD. I'D BEEN SENT THERE TO GET HER TO ANSWER STYLE QUESTIONS. ALL SHE WANTED TO TALK ABOUT WAS HER RECENT TRIP TO THAILAND FOR CHARITY.

HERE'S A PICTURE OF MILA, A BROTHEL SEX SLAVE I WAS ABLE TO SAVE. HER LIFE WAS A DISASTER.

WOW, UM... WHAT'S YOUR BIGGEST **FASHION** DISASTER?

AS I SCANNED MY QUESTIONS, I FELT HER SLIPPING AWAY.

THEN I DUG UP AN OLD TECHNIQUE.

I'M ALSO WORKING ON A BOOK ABOUT MY DAD.

OH? WHAT ABOUT?

ONCE AGAIN, MY DAD'S STORIES, WHICH WERE BECOMING *MY* STORY, MANAGED TO TURN A CONVERSATION AROUND.

WE FINISHED THE INTERVIEW. THAT SAME DAY, I FLEW BACK TO NEW YORK TO SEE BEN.

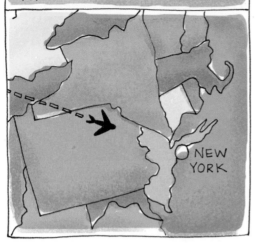

I DIDN'T ARRIVE UNTIL MIDNIGHT BUT HAD THE CAR SERVICE DROP ME OFF AT A NICE RESTAURANT IN SOHO, SO I COULD TELL BEN EVERY DETAIL OF MY INTERVIEW.

IT WAS SO GOOD TO SEE HIM! HE OPENED HIS ARMS AND FOLDED ME INTO A HUGE BEAR HUG.

OH MY GOD. THAT IS SO COOL. TELL ME MORE.

THEN I WAS LIKE, "WHAT'S YOUR BIGGEST FASHION DISASTER?"

LATER THAT NIGHT

MY GOD. THIS BODY!

HE MADE ME FEEL SO GOOD ABOUT MYSELF.

A WAY I COULD NEVER SEEM TO FEEL ON MY OWN.

FLAT CHEST

BIG EARS

INGROWN HAIR

KNOBBY KNEES

BEN FELL ASLEEP WITHIN MINUTES. I NEEDED HELP.

THE NEXT MORNING

I'D NEVER FELT SO CONFIDENT. SO PRETTY. SO SEXY. STILL, IN THE LIGHT OF DAY, WITHOUT WINE OR AMBIEN IN MY SYSTEM, THERE SEEMED TO BE SOMETHING MISSING.

I DIDN'T KNOW WHAT IT WAS. BUT I DIDN'T HAVE TO THINK ABOUT IT FOR LONG: HE LEFT THE NEXT DAY.

BY EVENING, I HAD FORGOTTEN MY MISGIVINGS. I FANTASIZED ABOUT THE IDYLLIC TIME WE'D HAD TOGETHER.

I FELL ASLEEP AT 2:30 A.M., WITH THE PHONE IN MY HAND, AFTER A MARATHON TALK WITH BEN.

AND TWO AMBIEN.

111

WHEN I WENT TO WORK ON MONDAY, I GOT AN E-MAIL FROM ASHLEY JUDD.

HOLY SHIT!

SHE SAID SHE'D ENJOYED MEETING ME AND THOUGHT I WAS BRAVE FOR WRITING ABOUT MY DAD. I WAS FLOATING ON AIR! *ASHLEY JUDD* HAD SENT *ME* A PERSONAL E-MAIL, UNRELATED TO WORK!

I E-MAILED BACK RIGHT AWAY, AND SHE E-MAILED ME BACK WITH *BOOK* RECOMMENDATIONS!

HA!

WHO'S THAT FROM?

OH, IT'S JUST ASHLEY JUDD. SHE E-MAILS ME SOMETIMES.

NO WAY!

WAY.

I LET IT SLIP TO MY EDITOR THAT ASHLEY JUDD AND I WERE SENDING E-MAILS BACK AND FORTH. SHE LET IT SLIP TO THE BOSS. SOON, I WAS DOING **ALL** THE CELEBRITY INTERVIEWS FOR THE MAGAZINE, FLYING ACROSS THE COUNTRY ON A MONTHLY BASIS, STAYING IN HOTELS WITH OVAL-SHAPED POOLS AND FLUFFY BATHROBES AND FIVE-THOUSAND-THREAD-COUNT SHEETS.

THE NIGHTLY PHONE CALLS WITH BEN TURNED INTO A FULL-FLEDGED LONG-DISTANCE RELATIONSHIP. I SAW HIM EVERY TIME I WAS IN L.A.

AND EVERY TIME I STARTED TO FEEL A PRICK OF DOUBT ABOUT HIM, IT WAS TIME TO LEAVE.

DOUBT

WITHIN MONTHS, I BECAME A REGULAR AT THE CHATEAU MARMONT HOTEL. SOMETIMES, THE GUYS AT THE FRONT DESK KNEW MY NAME AND UPGRADED ME TO A HUGE ONE-BEDROOM SUITE.

WELCOME BACK!

OTHER TIMES, THEY HAD NO IDEA WHO I WAS AND ACTED REALLY SNOBBY.

RIGHT AWAY, MR. GALLO.

AHEM.

THE ONE THING THAT MADE IT OK TO GO TO L.A. SO OFTEN WAS VISITING BEN. I WOULD HAVE BEEN SO LONELY AMONG THOSE FLASHY, FAKE PEOPLE WITHOUT HIM.

HIPSTER

B-LIST CELEBRITY

ASPIRING ACTOR

HANGER-ON

THE ONLY THING WAS I WAS KIND OF LONELY **WITH** HIM TOO.
I COULDN'T PUT MY FINGER ON THE REASON WHY.

HE WAS THE MOST THOUGHTFUL GUY I'D EVER MET.

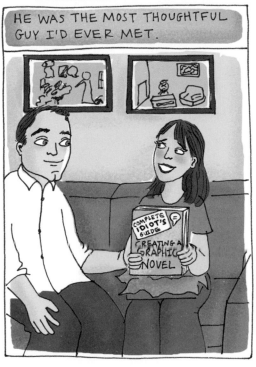

HE WAS GREAT IN BED.

HE'D READ MORE THAN ANYONE I'D EVER MET — PERHAPS EVEN MY FATHER.

I WAS 100 PERCENT **MYSELF** WITH HIM.

YET I TREATED THE RELATIONSHIP AS A CASUAL THING.

OH, NO, IT'S NOT SERIOUS.

MY FRIENDS COULDN'T UNDERSTAND MY HESITATION. WHEN I TRIED TO EXPLAIN MY DOUBTS, THEY SOUNDED RIDICULOUS.

"HE'S TOO CLEAN-CUT."

"HE INSISTS ON WEARING THESE HORRIBLE BLACK SHOES EVERY DAY."

"HIS CAR IS SO **BIG**."

TO ME, THOSE CHOICES SIGNALED A LACK OF POETRY IN HIS SOUL, A MARRIAGE TO THE CONCRETE.

TWO ON, TWO OUT. CLEMENS DEALS TO ORTIZ.

IT WAS A QUALITY THAT BOTH ATTRACTED AND REPULSED ME. IT WAS WHAT I IMAGINED I'D HAVE TO ACCEPT IF I EVER WANTED TO HAVE A HEALTHY RELATIONSHIP.

BUT I COULDN'T.

WHERE ARE YOU GOING?

I HADN'T YET KICKED MY ATTRACTION TO LARGER-THAN-LIFE NARCISSISTS, AND BEN WAS SO... WELL... *NORMAL.*

ONE ON, TWO OUT, ONE RUN IN. VARITEK STEPS TO THE PLATE.

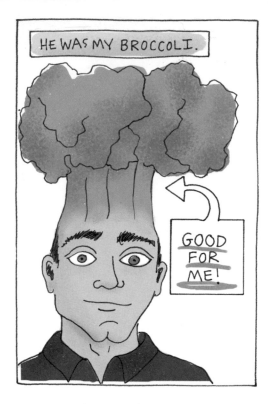

HE WAS MY BROCCOLI.

GOOD FOR ME!

WAS IT POSSIBLE I WASN'T IN LOVE WITH BEN BECAUSE HE WASN'T *ENOUGH* LIKE MY DAD? CHARMING... WILDLY PASSIONATE... MERCURIAL...

HE SAID, "YOU INSULTED THE UNIFORM OF THE REPUBLIC OF ARGENTINA!" I WAS IMMEDIATELY ARRESTED.

ALL I KNEW WAS THAT WHENEVER WE WERE APART, I MISSED BEN LIKE CRAZY.

BUT EVERY TIME WE SPENT MORE THAN A FEW DAYS TOGETHER, I FELT SUFFOCATED AND FOUND MYSELF PICKING ON HIM.

YOU'RE GOING TO WEAR *THAT* T-SHIRT?

AFTERWARD, I FELT TERRIBLE.

NO, YOU SHOULD WEAR IT. HONESTLY, IT LOOKS GREAT.

AND CONVINCED MYSELF OUR ISSUES WERE MY FAULT.

WHAT DO YOU MEAN, YOU DON'T WANT KIDS?

I DON'T HAVE THAT URGE; I LIKE MY LIFE THE WAY IT IS.

LUCKILY, THERE WERE SO MANY DISTRACTIONS IN L.A., I DIDN'T HAVE TO DEAL WITH MY FEELINGS FOR TOO LONG.

OOH, LOOK— KIRSTEN DUNST!

KITSON

IN MY SPARE TIME, I WAS STILL INVESTIGATING MY FATHER'S PAST.

MOST SATURDAYS, AT THE NEW YORK PUBLIC LIBRARY.

NEW LAPTOP

I FOUND MYSELF RELYING ON MY FATHER'S STORIES MORE AND MORE TO CONNECT WITH FAMOUS PEOPLE.

I'M ACTUALLY WORKING ON A BOOK ABOUT MY DAD. HE'S STILL MARRIED TO MY MOM, BUT I RECENTLY FOUND OUT HE'S A CON ARTIST.

LAURA DERN

TAPE RECORDER

FORGET ABOUT *MY* STORY — TELL ME *YOURS!*

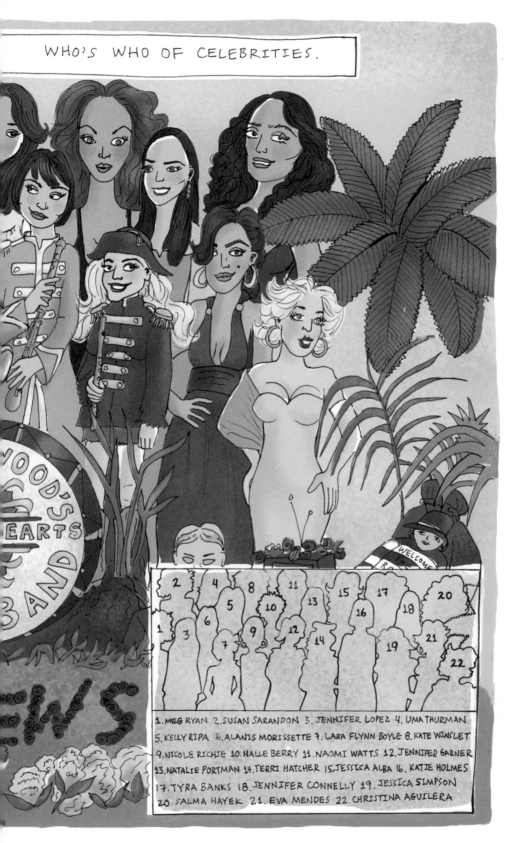

1. MEG RYAN 2. SUSAN SARANDON 3. JENNIFER LOPEZ 4. UMA THURMAN
5. KELLY RIPA 6. ALANIS MORISSETTE 7. LARA FLYNN BOYLE 8. KATE WINSLET
9. NICOLE RICHIE 10. HALLE BERRY 11. NAOMI WATTS 12. JENNIFER GARNER
13. NATALIE PORTMAN 14. TERRI HATCHER 15. JESSICA ALBA 16. KATIE HOLMES
17. TYRA BANKS 18. JENNIFER CONNELLY 19. JESSICA SIMPSON
20. SALMA HAYEK 21. EVA MENDES 22. CHRISTINA AGUILERA

THOUGH I AFFECTED INDIFFERENCE DURING INTERVIEWS, I WAS **DAZZLED** IN THE PRESENCE OF CELEBRITY. THERE WAS SOMETHING ABOUT BEING CHOSEN TO SIT DOWN WITH A PERSON WHO MILLIONS OF PEOPLE WANTED TO TALK TO, TO BE SEEN AT **HER** TABLE — AN INVITED GUEST — THAT WAS THRILLING FOR ME.

THE FEELING WAS FAMILIAR.

IT HAD BEEN A YEAR SINCE THE STORY ON MY FATHER HAD COME OUT, TWO YEARS SINCE WE'D SPOKEN. AT TIMES, I FORGOT THAT I **HAD** A REAL FATHER: HE EXISTED IN THE STORIES I TOLD ALONE.

YOU'RE **KIDDING**!

CATHERINE ZETA-JONES

FOR THE MOST PART, THAT DIDN'T BOTHER ME, EXCEPT DURING CERTAIN HOLIDAYS.

WHAT'S ALL THAT NOISE IN THE BACKGROUND?

WE'RE OUT TO DINNER FOR FATHER'S DAY. ARE YOU UPSET?

WHENEVER I MET MY MOTHER FOR LUNCH, I TOLD HER NOTHING ABOUT WHAT I WAS DOING AND ASKED NOTHING OF HER IN RETURN. SHE THOUGHT THE STORY WAS SAFELY PUT TO BED.

SO WHO ARE YOU INTERVIEWING NEXT?

DAD'S — I MEAN, NAOMI CAMPBELL.

IT WASN'T, OF COURSE. EVERY TIME I LIFTED THE LID ON MY FATHER'S LIFE, THOUSANDS OF CLUES CAME TUMBLING OUT, ONLY TO CREATE MORE QUESTIONS. BUT NOTHING ALLOWED ME TO YANK BACK THE WIZARD OF OZ-LIKE CURTAIN TO REVEAL HIS TRUE SELF.

I WANTED TO KNOW EVERYTHING. THIS ELUSIVE INFORMATION, I WAS SURE, HELD THE KEY TO MY FUTURE HAPPINESS. ALL THOSE MISSING PIECES, THE FEELING I DIDN'T BELONG, THE SUSPICION THAT I WAS DIFFERENT.... IT WOULD ALL MAKE SENSE.

BUT I NEEDED HELP.

A.R.M. ASSOCIATES, INC.

Albert R. McEvoy
President
Former Police Commissioner
Yonkers, New York
Licensed/Bonded/Insured
New York State

PRIVATE INVESTIGATIONS

Phone: 914-964-5734
Fax: 914-517-5900
Piarmassoc@aol.com
Post Office Box 147
Yonkers 10703

I THOUGHT ABOUT THE FILE THAT PI HAD TO HAVE ON MY FATHER, TWELVE INCHES THICK. I **HAD** TO HAVE THAT FILE.

HELLO?

HOW ARE YA? AL MCEVOY HERE.

AL! HELLO!

LISTEN, I'M SORRY I DIDN'T GET BACK TO YOU SOONER. I WAS IN FLORIDA PLAYING GOLF AND HADN'T CHECKED MY NEW YORK MESSAGES IN A WHILE.

SO DO YOU REMEMBER MY DAD?

OF COURSE, I DO. SEEMED LIKE AN INTERESTING GUY.

WE MADE A PLAN TO MEET THE FOLLOWING THURSDAY NIGHT.

LET'S MEET AT THE STAMFORD TRAIN STATION. WE CAN MEET ON THE PLATFORM.

WHAT WILL YOU LOOK LIKE?

YOU'LL KNOW ME. I LOOK LIKE A RETIRED COP.

THE DAY OF OUR MEETING, I RACED OUT OF WORK TO CATCH THE 5:53 P.M. TRAIN TO STAMFORD, FEELING LIKE I WAS STARRING IN A MOVIE ABOUT MY OWN LIFE.

IN THE RESTAURANT . . .

*Giulia, Dad's secretary
Jimmy B., ham radio
friend (has spina
bifida, in wheelchair)
Gustavo Torres, old friend
of my father's (stands
at least 6'7")
Marcus Kipplinger,
Dad's first cousin,
Mai Feng, my dad's
"email infatuation"
feng@hotmail.*

I HANDED HIM A LIST OF PEOPLE I
WANTED TO FIND.

I DID A PRELIMINARY SEARCH:
I'VE ALREADY FOUND THREE
OR FOUR LAWSUITS AGAINST
YOUR FATHER — AND ONE
AGAINST YOUR MOTHER — AS
WELL AS A BANK PROBLEM AND
AN APPLICATION FOR A LOAN.

WAIT A MINUTE —
THERE'S A LAWSUIT
FILED AGAINST
MY *MOTHER*?

YEAH, SOMETHING
TO DO WITH A
DINERS CLUB CARD
SHE DIDN'T PAY.

MY MOTHER WAS AN ABSOLUTE
SQUARE — SHE'D NEVER HAD SO
MUCH AS A PARKING TICKET.

129

OVER THE NEXT FEW WEEKS, AL TIED UP ALL THE LOOSE ENDS.

FEBRUARY 20, 2:35 P.M.: NO LUCK WITH MAI FENG — SORRY. ALL THE TRAILS WENT DEAD.

FEBRUARY 29, 5:19 P.M.: FOUND JIMMY B.!

MARCH 5, 1:23 P.M.: HERE'S GIULIA'S ADDRESS. GOOD LUCK.

HE'D SUGGESTED I SEND LETTERS TO THE PEOPLE HE WAS ABLE TO TRACK DOWN. I MAILED OFF THE LETTERS.

THE THREE LAWSUITS HE FOUND AGAINST MY PARENTS WERE FROM THE DINERS CLUB, THE GUY WHO'D BOUGHT OUR HOUSE AT AUCTION, AND A WALTER MATHESON OF CHAPPAQUA, NEW YORK.

ANY IDEA WHO THIS **MATHESON** GUY IS?

HE WAS MY MOM'S BEST FRIEND'S HUSBAND. I HADN'T SEEN HIM IN YEARS.

HI, GIRLS.

SEARCHING FOR THE TRUTH ABOUT MY FATHER WAS LIKE DIGGING AT THE BEACH. THE MORE I DUG, THE MORE THE HOLE KEPT FILLING UP WITH WATER.

WALTER, HOW ARE YA?

THE TOWEL

IN JUNE, BEN CAME TO VISIT ME IN NEW YORK. THE WEEKEND WAS GREAT, UNTIL . . .

BEN'S TOWEL

I FELT LIKE I WAS BEING CHOKED BY THAT TOWEL — I COULDN'T BREATHE.

DO YOU GET AN AIRPORT CONNECTION? I CAN'T SEE THE GODDAM BASEBALL SCORES.

WHERE DO YOU WANT TO GO TO DINNER TONIGHT?

BLUE RIBBON, MAYBE?

LATER THAT NIGHT AFTER SEVERAL GLASSES OF WINE, I FELT FLUSHED AND HAPPY.

BEFORE I CRAWLED INTO BED WITH HIM, I SECRETLY TOOK AMBIEN.

I DON'T KNOW WHY I HID IT FROM HIM — I'D TAKEN AMBIEN WITH HIS KNOWLEDGE BEFORE, DURING OUR ENDLESS PHONE CONVERSATIONS.

132

I DID IT AS A WAY TO FORCE MYSELF OFF OF THE PHONE WHEN I HAD TO WORK THE NEXT DAY. BUT IT DIDN'T ALWAYS WORK OUT THAT WAY. MOST OF THOSE AMBIEN-FUELED CONVERSATIONS HAD LED TO UNCONSCIOUS PHONE SEX.

I'M NAKED AND TOUCHING MYSELF...

WHICH I WAS REALLY GOOD AT, I HEAR.

I DID **WHAT** LAST NIGHT? NO, NO, I REMEMBER.

STILL, I SUPPOSE I KNEW HE WOULDN'T BE TOO KEEN ON THE IDEA OF ACTUAL SEX WITH A COMATOSE WOMAN.

JUST BEFORE I SCREWED THE CAP BACK ON, I LOOKED IN THE BOTTLE: I WAS DOWN TO MY LAST ONE! HOW HAD I RUN OUT SO QUICKLY?

DUANE READE
Ambien 10 mg.

THEN THE AMBIEN KICKED IN. I FELT DROWSILY HOT FOR HIM, WARM ALL OVER, AND, OF COURSE, EXPERIMENTAL.

WANNA GET ON THE FLOOR AND **SPANK** ME?

WHOA. OK.

DID YOU TAKE AMBIEN? YOU'RE ACTING WEIRD.

NO.

RIDE 'EM, COWBOY!

134

IN THE MORNING, I FELT ANXIOUS AGAIN.

YOU WERE GREAT LAST NIGHT.

THANKS ...?

I COULDN'T REMEMBER A **THING** THAT WE'D DONE — AFTER THE SPANKING, ANYWAY.

WE SPENT THE DAY LOUNGING AROUND MY APARTMENT. HE DIDN'T SAY A WORD ABOUT THE STATE I'D BEEN IN HOURS EARLIER.

FINALLY, I COULD NO LONGER PRETEND.

CONFUSED? WHAT DO YOU MEAN?

I LOVE YOU, BUT I'M NOT SURE I'M "IN LOVE" WITH YOU.

BUT THINGS HAVE BEEN GREAT BETWEEN US. WE JUST SPENT THE WHOLE DAY HANGING OUT. IT WAS BLISSFUL.

IT MAY HAVE BEEN BLISSFUL FOR YOU, BUT IT WASN'T FOR ME. I FELT . . . SUFFOCATED.

WE HAVE SOME PROBLEMS, BUT I'M WILLING TO OVER-LOOK THOSE THINGS, BECAUSE I LOVE YOU.

I LOVE YOU TOO, BUT ARE YOU WILLING TO OVERLOOK THE FACT THAT I MIGHT NOT BE *IN LOVE* WITH YOU?

I KNOW YOU HAVE ISSUES BECAUSE OF YOUR FATHER, AND HOPEFULLY, OVER TIME, YOU **WILL** FALL IN LOVE WITH ME.

BUT WHAT IF I DON'T?

I'M WILLING TO TAKE THAT RISK.

AND WHAT ABOUT THE FACT THAT YOU DON'T WANT TO HAVE CHILDREN? I NEVER ARGUE THAT POINT WITH YOU BECAUSE I'M UNSURE ABOUT OUR FUTURE.

IF THAT WAS SOMETHING YOU REALLY WANTED, I WOULDN'T ASK YOU TO GIVE THAT UP.

SO YOU'D HAVE KIDS YOU DIDN'T WANT?

FOR YOU, I WOULD.

AT DINNER THAT NIGHT, WE CHATTED ABOUT THE FOOD, THE WINE, THE PEOPLE AROUND US. IT WAS AS IF OUR PREVIOUS CONVERSATION HAD NEVER TAKEN PLACE. HOW COULD HE SAY HE WAS OK WITH THE FACT THAT I MIGHT NOT BE IN LOVE WITH HIM? OR BE WILLING TO BRING KIDS HE DIDN'T WANT INTO THE WORLD?

THAT NIGHT I SLEPT FITFULLY — I DIDN'T WANT TO TAKE MY LAST AMBIEN.

AS SOON AS HE LEFT FOR THE AIRPORT THE NEXT MORNING, THE TRAPPED SENSATION I'D BEEN FEELING ALL WEEKEND SUBSIDED.

I HAD TWO DIFFERENT DOCTORS CALL IN PRESCRIPTIONS FOR AMBIEN AND ASKED MY MOTHER, THE CONSUMMATE NONADDICT, TO SEND A FEW EXTRAS FROM HER BARELY USED STASH TO TIDE ME OVER.

HOW MANY DO YOU NEED?

UM, TEN OR SO? I'M NOT SURE WHEN I'LL BE ABLE TO GET TO THE PHARMACY.

IN NOVEMBER, BEN VISITED ME IN NEW YORK AGAIN. WE PLANNED TO SPEND A FEW DAYS TOGETHER, THEN TRAVEL TO HIS PARENTS' HOUSE IN BOSTON FOR THANKSGIVING. IT DIDN'T TAKE LONG FOR ME TO FEEL THE WALLS CLOSING IN.

IN CENTRAL PARK

AT DINNER

WHAT'S WRONG?

NOTHING.

THE NIGHT BEFORE WE LEFT FOR HIS PARENTS', THE FEELING INTENSIFIED. I WAS COOKING MY SPECIALTY, CHICKEN POT PIE.

I CAN'T DO THIS!

I THOUGHT I'D DONE THE RIGHT THING. I LOVED HIM, BUT I NEEDED TO BE **IN** LOVE. I WANTED TO FEEL MY STOMACH LURCH WHEN HE WAS AROUND; TO HAVE TROUBLE SLEEPING NOT BECAUSE I WAS MISERABLE BUT BECAUSE I WAS EXHILARATED; TO BE WILLING TO THROW MYSELF IN FRONT OF A TRUCK FOR HIM — OR **UNDER** ONE IF HE EVER LEFT ME.

THANKSGIVING 2005

AND YET, I WAS BACK WHERE I STARTED. THE MAN I WANTED TO KNOW — MY FATHER — WAS AS REMOTE FROM ME AS EVER. THE MAN CLOSEST TO ME, I'D JUST TOSSED OVERBOARD.

CONTACT

JUST AS AL MCEVOY HAD PREDICTED, I STARTED TO RECEIVE RESPONSES TO THE LETTERS I'D MAILED, LOOKING FOR CLUES TO MY PAST.

"YOUR LETTER CAME AS QUITE A SURPRISE."

WALTER MATHESON

I CALLED HIM.

ONE DAY, I GOT A PHONE CALL FROM YOUR DAD.

CAN YOU MEET ME BY THE DRESS BARN IN THE WHITE PLAINS MALL IN TWO HOURS?

WHAT'S THIS ALL ABOUT?

I'LL EXPLAIN LATER.

"GETTING A PHONE CALL OUT OF THE BLUE TO MEET AT A SECRET LOCATION. . . . . I HAVE TO ADMIT, IT WAS KIND OF EXCITING. I MEAN, I'M A **DENTIST**."

WHITE PLAINS MALL

A VERY GOOD BUSINESS DEAL HAS COME UP. HERE'S THE PROSPECTUS FOR THE COMPANY.

THE E.T.I. PROJECT

I'M GOING TO BE STRAIGHT WITH YOU. I NEED THIRTY THOUSAND DOLLARS TO BUY INTO THE COMPANY. I ALREADY HAVE SEVENTEEN THOUSAND DOLLARS OF THAT MONEY. WHAT I AM ASKING FROM YOU IS A LOAN FOR THE LAST THIRTEEN THOUSAND, IN EXCHANGE FOR ONE THOUSAND SHARES IN THE COMPANY. I CAN PAY YOU BACK IN TWO WEEKS.

WELL, I . . .

You know me. Our wives are old friends. And there is a very high likelihood this will make us both rich. So — what do you think?

You **GAVE** it to him?

I happened to have the money in my savings account. I wrote him a check on the spot. Driving home, I thought, what have I done?

"Two weeks went by, then six months. Finally, Barbara discovered the discrepancy in our bank books."

What's this?

SHE WAS REALLY ANGRY. BUT SHE'D BEEN FRIENDS WITH YOUR MOTHER SINCE HIGH SCHOOL, SO SHE DIDN'T WANT TO GET INVOLVED.

"WE STILL SAW YOUR PARENTS SOCIALLY. I NEVER BROUGHT UP THE MONEY BECAUSE YOUR FATHER ALWAYS BROUGHT IT UP FIRST."

THERE'S A BUSINESS DEAL COMING; YOUR MONEY IS ON THE WAY.

ALWAYS ANOTHER EXCUSE. FINALLY, I SAID, "ENOUGH," AND HANDED IT OVER TO AN ATTORNEY. IT TOOK TWO YEARS TO LITIGATE. IT BECAME VERY DIFFICULT FOR BARBARA TO STAY FRIENDS WITH YOUR MOM AFTER THAT.

LIKE MANY PEOPLE I'D SPOKEN TO, WALTER SEEMED TO FEEL ALMOST SORRY FOR MY FATHER.

YOUR DAD IS SUCH A SMART GUY. THERE WAS A TIME WHEN THINGS WERE GOING VERY WELL FOR HIM. HE HAD WHAT HE THOUGHT WAS THE MOST WONDERFUL JOB IN THE WORLD, AT RAMAPO COLLEGE. HE USED TO BRAG, "I WORK PART TIME; I HAVE A GREAT JOB WITH BENEFITS."

HE PAID CASH FOR THE HOUSE IN BRONXVILLE. AND I SAW SOME OF THE FURNITURE HE MADE — HE COULD HAVE MADE A GOOD LIVING AS A FURNITURE MAKER.

OVER THE NEXT MONTH, WALTER AND I SPOKE TWO MORE TIMES, AND HE ASKED ME TO SEND HIM A COPY OF MY ARTICLE ABOUT MY DAD. HE THANKED ME FOR SENDING IT, THEN OUR E-MAILS PETERED OUT. I WAS GLAD. I DIDN'T WANT TO STAY IN TOUCH: WHAT MY FATHER HAD DONE WAS TOO AWFUL.

145

I WAS BACK IN L.A. TO DO ANOTHER CELEBRITY INTERVIEW WHEN MY FATHER'S OLD FRIEND, GUSTAVO, CALLED.

SO, I KNOW YOU'RE STILL IN TOUCH WITH MY FATHER.

OH, HE CONSTANTLY SENDS ME POLITICAL ESSAYS.

THEN THIS MIGHT BE A LITTLE AWKWARD.

I HOPE YOU KNOW ME WELL ENOUGH TO LET YOUR GUARD DOWN AND TELL ME WHAT'S ON YOUR MIND.

AL MCEVOY HAD SUGGESTED I GIVE THE SMALLEST AMOUNT OF INFORMATION POSSIBLE TO GET SOMETHING BACK. BUT GUSTAVO WAS CRAFTY. HE ASKED JUST THE RIGHT QUESTIONS, AND I ENDED UP TELLING HIM ABOUT THE CREDIT CARDS, WALTER MATHESON, THE FORECLOSURE OF THE HOUSE.

COUPLE THINGS YOU NEED TO REALIZE. SOMEONE WHO HAS LIVED IN AS MANY DIFFERENT PLACES AS YOUR FATHER HAS... THERE'S ALWAYS BOUND TO BE PEOPLE TRYING TO GET AT HIM, TO SAY NEGATIVE THINGS.

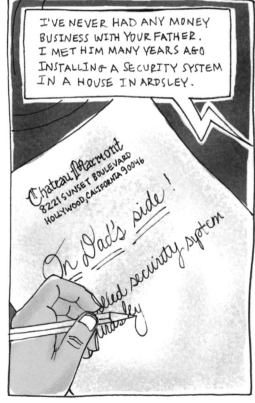

I'VE NEVER HAD ANY MONEY BUSINESS WITH YOUR FATHER. I MET HIM MANY YEARS AGO INSTALLING A SECURITY SYSTEM IN A HOUSE IN ARDSLEY.

146

I HEARD FROM JIMMY B., MY FATHER'S HAM RADIO FRIEND, ON THE DAY HE RECEIVED MY LETTER.

HI. WHAT'S UP?

AS YOU KNOW, MY FATHER AND I AREN'T SPEAKING. WELL, RECENTLY, IT'S BECOME REALLY IMPORTANT TO ME TO FIND OUT CERTAIN THINGS.

DOES HE HAVE ACCESS TO YOUR SOCIAL SECURITY NUMBER, BANK ACCOUNT NUMBERS, STUFF LIKE THAT?

SURE, I TRUST HIM TOTALLY.

DAYS AFTER THIS CONVERSATION, I RECEIVED AN E-MAIL FROM MARCUS KIPPLINGER, MY FATHER'S FIRST COUSIN WHO WORKED AS AN AP REPORTER IN WASHINGTON, D.C.

YOUR LETTER CAME AS QUITE A PLEASANT SURPRISE. TO GET TO YOUR QUESTION RIGHT AWAY, YOUR FATHER'S FATHER AND MY MOTHER WERE BROTHER AND SISTER. I LAST SAW YOUR DAD IN THE LATE 1950S OR EARLY 1960S.

LATER, WE CONNECTED ON THE PHONE.

SO, ARE YOU STILL IN TOUCH WITH ANYONE IN THE FAMILY?

JUST ELSA, REALLY. SHE LIVES IN BUENOS AIRES.

BINGO! MY FATHER'S HATED STEPSISTER!

I GOT AN IDEA ON THE SPOT.

YOU KNOW, I'D LOVE TO MEET HER. I'M PLANNING TO TRAVEL TO ARGENTINA THIS SUMMER.

SHE'S NOT IN THE BEST OF HEALTH. BUT I COULD CALL HER, I SUPPOSE.

MARCUS CALLED ME AGAIN TWO WEEKS LATER — JUST WHEN I WAS BEGINNING TO THINK ALL WAS LOST.

I'VE SPOKEN TO ELSA, AND SHE'S WILLING TO MEET YOU FOR COFFEE.

GREAT!

A FEW NIGHTS LATER . . .

RING! RING!

THE MAN'S VOICE WAS DEEP, ALMOST COMICALLY ITALIAN AMERICAN, LIKE A CHARACTER IN A GANGSTER FILM.

IS THIS THE DAUGHTER OF BILL SANDELL?

DID YOU SEND A LETTER TO GIULIA RUSSO?

YES.

GIULIA— MY FATHER'S SECRETARY! RUSSO MUST HAVE BEEN HER MARRIED NAME!

YES! I'VE BEEN WAITING TO HEAR FROM HER.

THE RUSSOS DON'T WANT NOTHIN' TO DO WITH NO SANDELLS.

CAN I ASK WHO THIS IS?

I WORK FOR GIULIA'S FATHER. I HAD SOME BUSINESS WITH YOUR FATHER ONCE. THAT'S ALL YOU NEED TO KNOW.

ARE YOU STILL IN TOUCH WITH HIM?

NO, HE DROPPED OFF THE RADAR.

IS YOUR FATHER STILL IN THE COUNTRY?

I DON'T KNOW. I HAVEN'T HAD CONTACT WITH HIM IN THREE YEARS.

WHAT ABOUT YOUR MOTHER?

LOOK, WHATEVER MY FATHER DID, I'M SURE MY MOTHER HAD NOTHING TO DO WITH IT.

YOUR MOTHER KNOWS EVERYTHING.

PLEASE JUST LET GIULIA KNOW I DON'T SPEAK TO MY FATHER, AND IF SHE EVER WANTS TO SAY HELLO, I'D LOVE TO TALK TO HER.

YOU CAN FORGET ABOUT THAT.

DIAL TONE

THE MINUTE I GOT OFF THE PHONE, I CALLED AL.

THAT'S GOTTA BE THE HUSBAND. IF HE KNOWS THAT MUCH, YOUR FATHER SCREWED GIULIA LIKE HE SCREWED THE OTHERS. IT CAN'T BE A JILTING SITUATION, BECAUSE YOUR FATHER WAS MARRIED. SO IF SHE WAS FOOLING AROUND WITH HIM, SHE KNEW IT WAS POTLUCK.

SO WHAT DO YOU THINK HE **DID**?

MAYBE HE APPLIED FOR A CREDIT CARD IN HER NAME. SHE THOUGHT SHE WAS WORKING FOR AN HONEST GUY AND FOUND OUT HE WAS A PHONY.

NOW I'LL **NEVER** HEAR FROM HER.

YOU STIRRED UP A LITTLE POT, WHICH IS WHAT WE WANTED TO DO. NOW WE'VE GOT TO MOVE ON.

THAT NIGHT, I HAD TO SIT ON MY HANDS TO NOT CALL BEN. EARLIER I'D FELT SUFFOCATED BY HIS DEPENDABILITY; NOW I WAS CRAVING IT. I DRANK A BOTTLE OF WINE BY MYSELF. I WANTED TO BLACK OUT, AND I DID. I'D DEAL WITH MY FEELINGS IN THE MORNING.

TWO TRUTHS AND A LIE

I HADN'T SEEN MY MOTHER IN MONTHS AND WANTED TO
LET HER IN ON SOME OF THE THINGS I'D DISCOVERED.
SECRETLY, I WAS HOPING SHE'D HEAR WHAT I HAD TO SAY,
BREAK DOWN, AND TELL ME EVERYTHING SHE KNEW. AT
THAT POINT, I WASN'T GOING TO GET THE TRUTH — OR
ANYTHING CLOSE TO IT — OUT OF MY FATHER. WHICH
MEANT IT HAD TO COME FROM HER.

GRAND CENTRAL STATION

ME

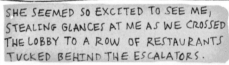

SHE SEEMED SO EXCITED TO SEE ME,
STEALING GLANCES AT ME AS WE CROSSED
THE LOBBY TO A ROW OF RESTAURANTS
TUCKED BEHIND THE ESCALATORS.

FIFTEEN MINUTES LATER . . .

I'D LIKE TO TALK TO YOU ABOUT SOMETHING.

ABOUT WHAT?

I'VE LEARNED MORE ABOUT DAD'S PAST.

I THOUGHT WE WERE GOING TO HAVE A NICE LUNCH.

SLAM

WELL, I'VE FOUND OUT A LOT.

LIKE WHAT?

153

I KNOW ABOUT THE PROBLEM WITH THE DINERS CLUB CARD.

I KNOW ABOUT THE LAWSUIT WALTER MATHESON BROUGHT AGAINST DAD.

HE AND DADDY DID A BUSINESS DEAL TOGETHER THAT DIDN'T WORK OUT.

IT'S ALL SETTLED — WALTER GOT BACK EVERY PENNY HE WAS OWED.

I KNOW ABOUT GIULIA.

WHAT DO YOU "KNOW" ABOUT GIULIA?

SHE WAS JUST A YOUNG GIRL — DADDY DID SOME BUSINESS WITH HER FATHER.

WELL, I WROTE HER A LETTER AND SOON AFTER GOT A THREATENING PHONE CALL FROM A MAN WHO WOULDN'T GIVE HIS NAME.

THREATENING?

HE SAID YOU KNEW EVERYTHING, AND I SHOULD ASK YOU WHAT HAPPENED BETWEEN DAD AND GIULIA.

I KNOW YOU THINK I'M TOTALLY NAIVE, BUT I'M NOT. I SEE WHAT GOES ON .... I CHOOSE TO GIVE DADDY THE BENEFIT OF THE DOUBT.

BUT THE EVIDENCE IS MOUNTING, MOM. DAD SEEMS TO BE DOING ILLEGAL THINGS. ARE YOU WILLING TO GIVE HIM THE BENEFIT OF THE DOUBT WHEN THERE IS **SO MUCH** DOUBT?

WELL, *I DON'T DOUBT HIM!*

ARGENTINA

I ARRIVED IN BUENOS AIRES WITH TWO OBJECTIVES: (1) SEE THE CITY WHERE MY FATHER WAS BORN; (2) MEET ELSA. I HAD HER PHONE NUMBER IN MY POCKET. IT WAS THE OFF-SEASON IN ARGENTINA. THE NIGHT I CHECKED IN, I WAS THE ONLY PERSON IN THE HOTEL. MALABIA HOUSE WAS BEAUTIFUL AND **CHEAP**.

AUGUST 2006

POWER OF THE DOLLAR

WITHIN TWENTY MINUTES, I'D UNPACKED MY BACKPACK, PLACED MY BALLED-UP SOCKS IN A DRAWER, AND HUNG MY T-SHIRTS ON HANGERS. THEN I PASSED OUT.

A FEW HOURS LATER, I HEADED OUTSIDE TO FIND DINNER.

WAS I IMAGINING IT, OR DID THE WOMEN IN THIS COUNTRY **LOOK** LIKE ME?

LATER THAT NIGHT...

I NEED SOME INFO ON GRANDPA'S GRAVE. I'M ALREADY IN ARGENTINA — WHY HAVEN'T YOU RESPONDED?

WHEN I REFRESHED MY BROWSER, I FOUND AN E-MAIL FROM BEN, TELLING ME HOW MUCH HE MISSED ME. HE SAID HE'D FINALLY GOTTEN FINANCING TO DIRECT A MOVIE HE'D WRITTEN, STARRING SOME OF THE BIGGEST NAMES IN HOLLYWOOD.

JUST SEEING HIS E-MAIL ADDRESS IN MY INBOX — SO FAMILIAR — INSTANTLY COMFORTED ME.

I WROTE BACK TO HIM RIGHT AWAY. I CONGRATULATED HIM AND DESCRIBED MY TRIP SO FAR.

THEN I CLICKED "SEND" AND STRETCHED OUT ON THE DIVAN, LISTENING TO THE HUM OF THE OVERHEAD LIGHT. NOW WHAT?

WHEN I WOKE UP, IT WAS LIGHT OUTSIDE. I DECIDED TO GO TO THE UNIVERSITY OF BUENOS AIRES TO LOOK UP MY FATHER'S RECORDS. NONE OF THE UNIVERSITIES HE'D CLAIMED TO HAVE ATTENDED HAD PANNED OUT. BUT HE HAD TO HAVE STUDIED **SOMEWHERE**.

MALABIA HOUSE OFFERED TO SET ME UP WITH A TRANSLATOR. RAYEN MET ME IN THE BREAKFAST ROOM WITH HER BOYFRIEND, JOE.

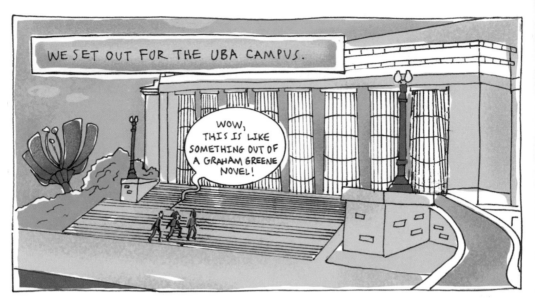

WE SET OUT FOR THE UBA CAMPUS.

WOW, THIS IS LIKE SOMETHING OUT OF A GRAHAM GREENE NOVEL!

OFICINA DE REGISTROS

SHE SAYS ALL THE RECORDS ARE HERE, BUT SHE CAN ONLY SHOW THEM TO THE PEOPLE THEY BELONG TO.

TEN MINUTES LATER...

THERE'S NO RECORD OF YOUR FATHER. SHE CHECKED ALL THE WAY BACK TO THE FIFTIES.

I WAS DISAPPOINTED AND, FRANKLY, I IMPRESSED. HOW HAD HE TAUGHT COLLEGE-LEVEL ECONOMICS WITHOUT AN EDUCATION?

THAT AFTERNOON, I CALLED MY FATHER'S STEPSISTER, ELSA.

ALO?

ELSA?

WE MADE A PLAN TO MEET LATER IN THE WEEK.

160

I SPENT THE NEXT FEW DAYS OF MY TRIP SIGHTSEEING.

I SAW THE PINK HOUSE.

CLICK!

I WATCHED A TANGO PERFORMANCE.

CLAP CLAP CLAP

I STROLLED THROUGH THE MARKET OF SAN TELMO.

EVERYWHERE I LOOKED, I SAW SIGNS OF MY FATHER.

CARLOS GARDEL

ON THURSDAY, I MET ELSA IN FRONT OF MY HOTEL. SHE WASN'T ANYTHING LIKE THE MONSTER I'D EXPECTED.

THE SMOG IS TERRIBLE TODAY.

I STUDIED HER FROM THE SIDE. HALF HER FACE APPEARED PARALYZED, HER EYE DROOPED, AND ONE SIDE OF HER MOUTH WAS TURNED DOWN. SHE MENTIONED HER CONDITION REFLEXIVELY, AS IF TO BEAT ME TO THE PUNCH.

I HAD A VIRUS. NOW MY FACE LOOKS TERRIBLE, TERRIBLE.

AS WE DROVE THROUGH THE CITY, SHE POINTED OUT SIGHTS.

THIS IS A STATUE OF GENERAL JOSÉ DE SAN MARTÍN.

THIS IS THE CITY HOSPITAL.

IS THE HOSPITAL ANY GOOD?

OF COURSE NOT. IT IS TERRIBLE. I HAVE A PRIVATE DOCTOR. IT IS THE ONLY WAY.

SHE TOLD ME ABOUT HER CHILD-HOOD IN VIENNA AND THE GATED COMMUNITY IN BUENOS AIRES SHE'D GROWN UP IN AFTER MY GRANDFATHER MARRIED HER MOTHER.

WE CAN HAVE LUNCH AT THE CLUB.

HER ENTITLED HAUTEUR GAVE ME INSIGHT: SHE HAD GOTTEN TOO MUCH AND MY FATHER TOO LITTLE.

SO YOU GREW UP WITH MY FATHER, RIGHT?

HE HAD HIS LIFE, AND I HAD MINE.

I WAS JUST WONDERING. WE DON'T SPEAK.

OH, REALLY? THAT'S TOO BAD.

SHE QUICKLY CHANGED THE SUBJECT.

THERE'S THE FOOTBALL STADIUM. AH, AND THERE'S THE CLUB.

163

SHE LED ME TO THE DINING ROOM, WITH ITS HIGH CEILINGS AND ENORMOUS ROUND TABLES, AND WE SAT BY A WINDOW, OVERLOOKING AN EXPANSIVE GREEN LAWN.

A COURSE FOR THE HORSES.

OK, BUT I USUALLY DON'T. NO ONE SMOKES IN THE STATES ANYMORE.

ACH— I AM STILL HERE!

OVER LUNCH, WE MADE LIGHT CONVERSATION ABOUT OUR LIVES.

SO WHERE DO YOU LIVE?

IN A VERY NICE NEIGHBORHOOD.

ALONE?

WITH MY SON, MANUEL.

THE SMALL TALK WAS EXCRUCIATING. I WAS CIRCLING AROUND THE QUESTIONS I REALLY WANTED TO ASK. SHE WAS THE ONLY PERSON I KNEW WHO'D KNOWN MY FATHER BEFORE ALL THE LIES.

WHAT WAS MY FATHER LIKE AS A CHILD?

WHAT DOES HE DO?

WHY DOES HE HATE YOU SO MUCH?

OH, HE'LL BE FINISHING SCHOOL FOR THE REST OF HIS LIFE.

WHY ALL THE LIES?

WAS HE EVER DIFFERENT?

MY FATHER DESCRIBED HIS FATHER AS EXTREMELY BRILLIANT AND CONNECTED. IS THAT TRUE?

YES, YES — HE WAS EXTREMELY EDUCATED.

DO YOU HAPPEN TO KNOW WHY MY FATHER LEFT ARGENTINA?

YES, I DO.

STUB STUB STUB

HE DESERTED THE ARMY. THEY CAME LOOKING FOR HIM. A VERY NICE OFFICER ASKED MY FATHER IF YOUR FATHER WAS HIDING IN THE HOUSE. HE WASN'T ANYWHERE TO BE FOUND. HE LATER CALLED, AND MY FATHER GOT HIM OUT OF THE COUNTRY, INTO PARAGUAY.

165

THAT'S ALL I KNOW — AND THAT'S ALL I **WANT** TO KNOW.

ALL THE WOMEN IN MY FATHER'S LIFE SEEMED TO CLOSE THEIR EYES.

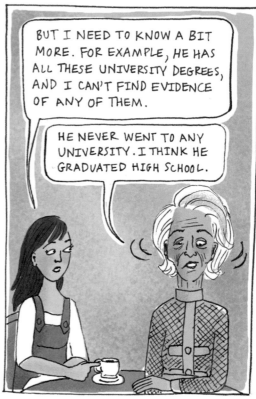

BUT I NEED TO KNOW A BIT MORE. FOR EXAMPLE, HE HAS ALL THESE UNIVERSITY DEGREES, AND I CAN'T FIND EVIDENCE OF ANY OF THEM.

HE NEVER WENT TO ANY UNIVERSITY. I THINK HE GRADUATED HIGH SCHOOL.

BUT HIS EDUCATION HAD TO COME FROM SOMEWHERE —

IT WAS A REALLY GOOD CATHOLIC BOARDING SCHOOL, RIGHT?

BOARDING SCHOOL? NO.

DO YOU REMEMBER WHICH SCHOOL HE WENT TO?

THE ONLY ONE THAT WOULD TAKE HIM!

AT THAT, I TOLD HER ABOUT MY CONVERSATION WITH THE DEAN OF THE COMMUNITY COLLEGE AND HOW I'D FOUND OUT MY FATHER'S CREDENTIALS WERE FORGED.

I WOULD HAVE HOPED HE HAD CHANGED BY NOW.

167

HAVE YOU EVER MET HER?

ONLY IN THE LAST YEAR OF HER LIFE. THEY WERE ESTRANGED UNTIL THEN.

SO WHEN IS THE LAST TIME YOU SAW MY FATHER?

AFTER MY FATHER DIED.

HE COMMITTED SUICIDE, YOU KNOW.

YES, I KNOW.

RIGHT AFTERWARD, YOUR FATHER CAME TO ARGENTINA AND TRIED TO GET MONEY FROM ME.

SERIOUSLY?

MY FATHER OWNED A FACTORY THAT WAS DOING VERY WELL. BUT YOUR FATHER COULDN'T TOUCH THE MONEY. BECAUSE EARLIER, HE HAD CLEANED OUT A BANK ACCOUNT OF MY FATHER'S.

WHEN?

I DON'T KNOW; WHEN HE WAS YOUNGER. IT BROKE MY FATHER'S HEART.

THERE WERE RARE TIMES WHEN THE EMOTION MY FATHER SHOWED SEEMED GENUINE; ONE OF THEM WAS WHEN HE TALKED ABOUT HIS FATHER. SO I FOUND THIS NEWS SHOCKING.

"THE MINUTE YOUR FATHER HEARD ABOUT HIS FATHER'S DEATH, HE CAME TO ARGENTINA."

SELL THE FACTORY AND GIVE ME MY HALF!

ABSOLUTELY NOT.

"I HAD A BRIEFCASE FULL OF PAPERS IN THE LIVING ROOM. I WENT INTO THE OTHER ROOM, AND WHEN I RETURNED, THE BRIEFCASE WAS GONE, AND SO WAS HE."

"BUT HE TOOK THE WRONG ONE! I'D ALREADY GIVEN THE *REAL* BRIEFCASE — WITH THE PAPERS THAT PROVED OWNERSHIP OF THE FACTORY — TO MY HUSBAND TO HIDE, BECAUSE I THOUGHT HE MIGHT TRY SOMETHING LIKE THAT."

I NEVER SAW HIM AGAIN.

IF HE RANG MY DOORBELL TODAY, I WOULDN'T LET HIM IN.

I FELT A SUDDEN URGE TO PROTECT MY FATHER FROM THIS WOMAN WHO CLEARLY HATED HIM. BUT THE DRIVE TO PRESS ON WAS *STRONGER*.

DO YOU HAPPEN TO KNOW WHY HE CHANGED HIS NAME? BECAUSE MY LAST NAME IS SANDELL.

SOMETHING TO DO WITH A BANK HE WAS WORKING FOR IN NEW YORK.

HE'S BEEN RUNNING FROM "SCHMIDT" EVER SINCE.

THE NEXT DAY, ELSA TOOK ME TO A MUSEUM OF MODERN ART IN LA BOCA, A COLORFUL WATERFRONT *BARRIO*.

DO YOU OWN A LOT OF ART?

OH, YES. I HAVE SOME OF HIS AND SOME OF HIS TOO.

I DON'T HAVE THE WALL SPACE FOR IT ALL. I WILL HAVE TO SELL SOME.

BACK AT THE HOTEL...

I KNEW I SHOULDN'T CALL BEN, GIVEN MY HISTORY OF AMBIVALENCE ABOUT HIM.

BUT I WAS LONELY IN THAT NEARLY EMPTY HOTEL, MY ONLY COMPANY THE OCCASIONAL SOUND OF A MAID'S FOOTSTEPS.

SO WHAT HAS FILMING BEEN LIKE?

FORGET ABOUT THAT — I WANT TO HEAR ABOUT ELSA!

WE TALKED FOR HOURS. IT FELT SO GOOD TO HAVE SOMEONE TO SHARE ALL THIS WITH. AND NOT JUST SOMEONE — **BEN.**

YOU'RE KIDDING! SHE ACTUALLY **SAID** THAT?

FOR MONTHS I'D FELT UNMOORED, ADRIFT.

GOD, I CAN'T BELIEVE YOU'VE BEEN HAVING SUCH CRAZY ADVENTURES.

UNSEEN.

TELL ME MORE. I CAN'T GET ENOUGH!

BY THE END OF THE NIGHT, I FELT LIKE I EXISTED AGAIN.

THE NEXT DAY, I HIRED A DRIVER TO TAKE ME TO MEMORIAL CEMETERY, WHERE MY GRANDFATHER WAS BURIED. IT LOOKED LIKE A COUNTRY CLUB.

A BLONDE WOMAN DROVE ME OUT TO THE PLOT IN A LITTLE GOLF CART.

SHE STOOD RESPECTFULLY TO ONE SIDE AS I SNAPPED A PICTURE.

AFTERWARD, I HAD THE DRIVER
TAKE ME TO RECOLETA, ONE OF
THE WEALTHIEST NEIGHBORHOODS
IN BUENOS AIRES, TO LOOK AT MY
GRANDFATHER'S FORMER HOME.

THEN WE DROVE TO ELSA'S
APARTMENT. THE NEIGHBORHOOD
WAS EQUALLY POSH. TOO NERVOUS
TO GET OUT OF THE CAR, I ROLLED
DOWN THE WINDOW AND SNAPPED
A PICTURE FROM THE FRONT SEAT.

ALL I SAW, WHEN I LOOKED AT
THE HOUSE, WAS EVERYTHING MY
FATHER HAD BEEN DENIED. IT WAS
A HOUSE — AND A LIFE — THAT
MADE HIM PRETEND TO BE
EVERYTHING HE WASN'T.

Contract of Denial

A FEW DAYS AFTER I RETURNED TO NEW YORK, I GOT A PHONE CALL FROM MY MOTHER.

WHY ARE YOU WHISPERING?

I'M IN THE BACKYARD— SO DADDY WON'T HEAR.

I COULD HEAR HER FUMBLING WITH A PIECE OF PAPER.

I WROTE A FEW THINGS DOWN, SO I COULD REMEMBER WHAT I WANTED TO SAY.

I KNOW YOU WENT TO ARGENTINA.

IT'S TRUE.

I KNOW YOU MET ELSA.

ALSO TRUE.

SHE STARTED TO CRY.

SOME PEOPLE LIKE TO SPILL THEIR GUTS.

I'M NOT LIKE THAT. I'M MORE OF A PRIVATE PERSON.

I KNOW YOU ARE, BUT—

I THINK PARENTS HAVE THE RIGHT TO TAKE CERTAIN THINGS TO THE GRAVE.

I RESPECT THAT, MOM. BUT THE THINGS YOU'RE REFERRING TO AFFECTED ME DIRECTLY. SO PRIVACY ISN'T THE ISSUE HERE.

YOUR FIRST LOYALTY SHOULD BE TO THE FAMILY.

174

IT WAS A REFRAIN. SOMETHING MY MOTHER HAD BEEN SAYING SINCE I WAS A KID. BUT THIS LOYALTY HAD COST ME DEARLY. FOR IT, I'D SACRIFICED SO MANY THINGS: TRUST IN MEN. MY ABILITY TO LOVE. A CLEAN CREDIT REPORT. MY VERY SENSE OF SELF. THE TRUTH WAS MORE IMPORTANT THAN LOYALTY.

I DON'T WANT YOU TO RUIN MY LIFE.

RUIN YOUR LIFE?

BECAUSE I HAVE A CHILD WHO'S GOING TO EXPOSE MY LIFE, AND I DON'T THINK I'M STRONG ENOUGH TO JUST WALK AWAY FROM MY HUSBAND.

WHO IS ASKING YOU TO WALK AWAY?

LAURIE . . . JUST STOP.

I CAN'T STOP.

The Price of Fiction

MY MOTHER ARRANGED A MEETING. SHE PICKED ME UP AT THE TRAIN STATION AND DROVE ME TO MY PARENTS' HOUSE. NEITHER OF US SAID MUCH ON THE DRIVE THERE.

OH! I MISSED THE TURN.

WHEN I WALKED INTO THE HOUSE, I SAW MY FATHER STANDING IN THE LIVING ROOM.

IT'S BEEN A LONG TIME, LAURIE. THREE AND A HALF YEARS.

TEARS WELLED, BUT I BLINKED THEM BACK. I WAS DETERMINED TO HOLD ON TO MY HARD-WON STOICISM.

YES, IT HAS.

MY FATHER LOOKED DIFFERENT. ONE SIDE OF HIS MUSTACHE WAS LONGER THAN THE OTHER, AND HE WAS HEAVIER THAN USUAL.

AH... WHY DON'T YOU SIT THERE?

OOF.

FOR A FEW MINUTES, HE SAID NOTHING.

THEN...

EVERYONE KNOWS ABOUT THE DEGREES. I WAS AT A FAMILY PARTY AND FOUND OUT YOU'D SPOKEN TO AUNT OLIVE. YOU'D SPOKEN TO COUSIN LISA. YOU'D SPOKEN TO BOTH OF YOUR SISTERS. AND YOU'D TOLD COUSIN ROSE, WHO TOLD HER HUSBAND, DAN, AND, STUPID ASSHOLE THAT HE WAS, HE TOLD THE REST OF THE FAMILY. I WAS THE LAST TO KNOW.

I STILL WANTED TO BELIEVE HE WAS CAPABLE OF LOVE.

LIFE IS SHORT, DAD, AND WHO KNOWS HOW MANY YEARS YOU HAVE LEFT. DO YOU REALLY WANT YOUR LEGACY TO BE A PACK OF LIES, WHEN THE REAL YOU IS FAR MORE INTERESTING?

THIS WAS IT: ONE LAST CHANCE TO LET GO OF HIS FICTIONS. ONE LAST CHANCE TO BE A FATHER. I DIDN'T HAVE IT IN ME TO OFFER HIM MORE THAN THAT.

WHY DON'T YOU LET US LOVE **YOU** BY BEING WHO YOU REALLY ARE?

I'LL TELL YOU WHO I REALLY AM: I AM ONE OF THE MOST ERUDITE, EDUCATED, AND CULTURED MEN YOU WILL EVER MEET. I KNOW PEOPLE WHO HAVE **FIVE** PHDs WHO AREN'T AS SMART AS I AM.

182

SO YOU'D RATHER GO TO THE GRAVE WITH YOUR SECRETS.

WHAT DOES IT MATTER? WHEN I DIE, YOU'LL FORGET ABOUT ME ANYWAY.

ALL FINISHED HERE? LAURIE, WHAT TIME IS YOUR TRAIN?

THE NEXT ONE IS AT EIGHT TWENTY PM.

YOU'D BETTER TAKE HER NOW.

WE STOOD UP. I HUGGED MY FATHER GOOD-BYE. THE GESTURE WAS PERFUNCTORY AND BRISK, THE EQUIVALENT OF A HANDSHAKE BETWEEN STRANGERS.

I WASN'T SURE I'D HEARD HER CORRECTLY: WAS SHE TIRED OF LIVING A LIE TOO? HAD SHE BEEN MORE SUPPORTIVE OF ME THAN ANYONE KNEW?

YOU ARE? WHY?

BECAUSE I DON'T CARE WHO HE IS. I STILL LOVE HIM.

HER LAST WORDS SEEMED TO HANG IN THE AIR. THEY WERE PROOF POSITIVE SHE WAS NEVER GOING TO CHANGE.

Metro-North Railroad

THAT WAS OK. SHE WASN'T THE ONE WHO NEEDED TO.

Metro-North Railroad

Good-bye, DOUBT

I WAS IN TORONTO TO DO AN-
OTHER INTERVIEW. WHEN I
RETURNED TO MY HOTEL ROOM,
I DIALED BEN.

I'M SO GLAD WE TALKED WHEN I WAS IN ARGENTINA. I MISS YOU.

I MISS YOU TOO.

I WANT TO TRY AGAIN.

LAURIE...

IT SEEMED SO CLEAR TO ME. BEN WAS THE ONLY PERSON WHO HAD EVER FULLY ACCEPTED ME. THE ONLY ONE WHO'D SEEMED TO LOVE ME FOR EXACTLY WHO I WAS — EVEN WHEN I WASN'T SURE WHO THAT WAS.

I MEAN IT! I LOVE YOU. IT'S JUST THAT I'VE NEVER BEEN ABLE TO TRUST ANYONE BECAUSE OF MY FUCKED-UP CHILDHOOD.

YOU KNOW I WANT THAT TOO, BUT...

IN THAT MOMENT, I FORGOT ALL MY RESERVATIONS ABOUT BEN. HIS PASSIVITY; HIS REFUSAL TO TALK ABOUT OUR RELATIONSHIP UNLESS WE WERE ON THE VERGE OF BREAKING UP; HIS RELUCTANCE TO BE A DAD; HIS DENIAL ABOUT MY AMBIVALENCE TOWARD HIM. ALL I KNEW WAS THAT I WANTED HIM.

BUT WHAT?

WHERE IS THIS COMING FROM? IS THIS BECAUSE I'M LESS AVAIL-ABLE NOW, WITH THE MOVIE?

YOU KNOW THIS HAS NOTHING TO DO WITH THE MOVIE!

I'M TALKING ABOUT THE FACT THAT I'M SO **BUSY** NOW. I'M NOT AVAILABLE. AND NOW YOU WANT ME.

NO! PLEASE, LET'S GIVE IT ONE MORE SHOT. JUST ONE. LET ME COME OUT THERE AND VISIT YOU AND PROVE TO YOU THAT I REALLY MEAN WHAT I SAY.

IT WOULD BE BETTER IF I CAME TO NEW YORK.

YES! CAN YOU COME SOON?

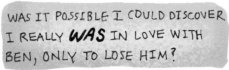

WAS IT POSSIBLE I COULD DISCOVER I REALLY **WAS** IN LOVE WITH BEN, ONLY TO LOSE HIM?

FIFTEEN MINUTES LATER, I DIDN'T HAVE TO THINK ABOUT IT.

TWO DAYS LATER, BEN VISITED ME IN NEW YORK.

LET'S NEVER BREAK UP AGAIN.

A Storybook Life

IN APRIL, I WAS SENT TO NASHVILLE TO INTERVIEW ASHLEY JUDD AGAIN. A CAR SERVICE TOOK ME TO FRANKLIN, TENNESSEE. WE PASSED MILES OF FARMLAND, COWS AND HORSES, WINDING ROADS.

WE PULLED UP TO A MASSIVE MANSION SET ON TWO HUNDRED ACRES OF LAND.

I SAT DOWN IN HER SUNROOM: IT WAS FILLED WITH FLORAL COUCHES, GARDENING BOOKS, AND FRAMED FAMILY PORTRAITS.

SHE'LL BE DOWN IN A MINUTE.

FIFTEEN MINUTES LATER, ASHLEY WALKED INTO THE ROOM.

HELLO! DID YOU HAVE A GOOD TRIP? LET'S GO OUTSIDE.

SHE PREPARED TWO BOWLS OF HOMEMADE ICE CREAM AND SPREAD A BLANKET ON THE GRASS. HER DOG AND CAT FROLICKED AROUND US AS WE LAY ON THE BLANKET, LOOKING OVER MILES OF ROLLING GREEN PASTURE.

THOSE ARE MY BLUEBELLS; I PLANTED THEM MYSELF.

189

BETWEEN BITES OF ICE CREAM, I ASKED HER QUESTIONS. I WAS THERE TO INTERVIEW HER FOR A BEAUTY FEATURE. HER ANSWERS WERE BIZARRE.

SO, WHAT'S YOUR BIGGEST BEAUTY SECRET?

SERENITY.

TAPE RECORDER

OK, UM, WHAT'S ONE BEAUTY PRODUCT YOU NEVER LEAVE THE HOUSE WITHOUT?

MY HIGHER POWER.

IS THAT A SPECIFIC BRAND? BECAUSE WE NEED TO BE ABLE TO CALL THESE ITEMS IN AND SHOOT THEM.

OK, SO WHAT WOULD BE YOUR GO-TO BEAUTY TIP?

GO TO REHAB FOR DEPRESSION.

SHUFFLE SHUFFLE

SHE ENDED UP TELLING ME THE STORY OF HOW SHE'D VISITED HER SISTER AT A REHAB CENTER IN TEXAS, WHERE SHE WAS BEING TREATED FOR OVEREATING, AND WOUND UP CHECKING HERSELF IN, FOR DEPRESSION, ANGER, AND ISSUES OF CODEPENDENCE.

YOU WENT TO **REHAB** FOR DEPRESSION?

I DID, AND IT CHANGED MY LIFE. NOW, MY WORST DAY IS BETTER THAN MY BEST DAY BEFORE REHAB.

BUT HOW COULD YOU POSSIBLY GET DEPRESSED, LIVING THIS LIFE?

SHE TOLD ME ABOUT HER UPBRINGING, WHICH SOUNDED POSITIVELY GOTHIC: THIRTEEN DIFFERENT SCHOOLS IN TWELVE YEARS. ABUSE. ALCOHOLISM. CONSTANT MOVING AROUND. MY OWN UPBRINGING, BY COMPARISON, SEEMED LIKE **FATHER KNOWS BEST.**

SHE'D UNKNOWINGLY PLANTED A SEED.

BEN AND I WERE TALKING AGAIN ON A NIGHTLY BASIS.

I'M PULLING INTO IN-N-OUT BURGER....HANG ON.

BUT THINGS HAD CHANGED. I WANTED TO DIVE INTO INTIMACY. HE WASN'T READY.

I WANT TO COME TO L.A. FOR YOUR BIRTHDAY.

I DON'T KNOW IF THAT'S A GOOD IDEA.

I BOOKED A TICKET ANYWAY.

I THOUGHT WE DISCUSSED THIS.

IF WE'RE GOING TO BE IN A RELATIONSHIP, THEN WE NEED TO BE IN A RELATIONSHIP. I'M SICK OF THIS LONG-DISTANCE BULLSHIT.

BUT WHEN I WENT TO L.A., I MET A DIFFERENT BEN.

SO THEN I TOLD SYLVIE... BEN—ARE YOU LISTENING?

YEAH, BABE, I JUST HAVE TO CHECK MY E-MAILS BECAUSE I'M WAITING FOR A MESSAGE FROM MY MANAGER.

HANG ON. I'VE GOT TO READ THIS. WHAT THE FUCK? THIS IS REDONKULOUS!

REDONKULOUS?!

THE VISIT WAS NEARLY UNBEARABLE.

WHAT DO YOU THINK A HEART ATTACK FEELS LIKE?

I DON'T KNOW...

ON MY LAST NIGHT IN L.A., WE WENT TO SEE A MOVIE. IT WAS A POOR CHOICE: THE MOVIE, ABOUT DAMAGED RELATIONSHIPS, SEEMED TO HIGHLIGHT EVERY ISSUE WE WERE HAVING.

I LOOKED AT THE PROFILE OF HIS FACE IN THE DARK: I HAD TO BREAK UP WITH HIM NOW! I COULDN'T WAIT ANOTHER MINUTE! THEN I TOOK A BREATH. NO, I WAS JUST PROJECTING. WHAT WAS BEING PLAYED OUT UP THERE HAD NOTHING TO DO WITH US.

I PUT MY HAND ON HIS ARM AND STROKED IT. HE DIDN'T MOVE. HE WAS IGNORING ME! I WAS BEING ABANDONED!

WHERE ARE YOU GOING?

TO THE BATHROOM.

I TOOK THREE DEEP BREATHS AND LOOKED AT MY REFLECTION.

CALM DOWN.

LATER THAT NIGHT...

I THINK I SHOULD MOVE TO L.A.

I'M NOT READY FOR THAT.

THIS CONFIRMS EVERYTHING I EVER SUSPECTED! YOU WERE CHASING ME BECAUSE YOU COULDN'T HAVE ME!

THAT'S BULLSHIT!

THAT NIGHT, WE WENT THROUGH THE MOTIONS OF "CUDDLING," BUT WE WERE EACH IN OUR OWN WORLD. (AND I WAS, LITERALLY.) THOSE EARLY WORDS OF BEN'S HAUNTED ME: "THE MOST LONELY I'VE EVER FELT WAS WHEN I WAS IN A RELATIONSHIP THAT WASN'T WORKING."

Blackout

I OPENED MY E-MAIL TO FIND A MESSAGE FROM ASHLEY.

HEY, GIRL, HOW ARE YOU?

MAYBE IT'S BECAUSE SHE'D CONFIDED IN ME OR BECAUSE I WAS ENAMORED WITH HER ASHLEY-JUDD-NESS, I DON'T KNOW, BUT I FOUND MYSELF TELLING HER EVERYTHING THAT HAD BEEN GOING ON IN MY LIFE.

I'M MISERABLE.... I'M FIGHTING WITH MY BOYFRIEND.... I THINK I MIGHT BE ADDICTED TO AMBIEN.

WHAT I DIDN'T TELL HER WAS THE EXTENT OF MY ADDICTION. FIVE MILLIGRAMS OF AMBIEN ONCE A WEEK ON SUNDAY NIGHTS HAD TURNED INTO FIFTEEN TO TWENTY MILLIGRAMS NIGHTLY.

THOUGH THE LABEL HAD WARNED NOT TO MIX IT WITH ALCOHOL, I DRANK FREELY. SOMETIMES I WASHED DOWN A PILL WITH A SIP OF RED WINE.

"SLEEP-EATING" WAS A KNOWN SIDE EFFECT OF AMBIEN: I HAD STARTED WAKING UP WITH PREPARED PLATES OF FOOD IN MY BED.

CHEESE. CRACKERS. KNIFE. (HEY, AT LEAST I WAS CLASSY.)

I ONCE WOKE UP TO FIND A POT OF SOUP OVER AN OPEN FLAME ON THE STOVE.

PERHAPS I ATE MORE AT NIGHT BECAUSE I'D ALL BUT **STOPPED** EATING DURING THE DAY. I WASN'T DOING IT TO LOSE WEIGHT; I JUST WASN'T INTERESTED IN FOOD.

BEER

CHAMPAGNE

BUTTER

AND THEN THERE WERE THOSE TWO INCIDENTS I'D NEVER SPOKEN OF TO ANYONE . . .

IN THE WEEKS AFTER I'D BROKEN UP WITH BEN THE FIRST TIME, I'D TAKEN A BATH, TRYING TO SOOTHE MYSELF. IT WAS CLOSE TO BEDTIME, SO I'D POPPED A FEW AMBIEN.

201

HAVE YOU EVER CONSIDERED IN-PATIENT TREATMENT?

SHE SENT ME A LINK TO THE PLACE SHE'D GONE: WWW.SHADESOFHOPE.COM

THANKS — I'LL THINK ABOUT IT.

I HAD NO INTENTION OF THINKING ABOUT IT.

BUT THEN...

ASHLEY JUDD SUGGESTED I CALL.... I CAN'T STOP TAKING AMBIEN. I'M DRINKING EVERY NIGHT OF THE WEEK.

WE SPOKE FOR FORTY-FIVE MINUTES. THE WOMAN ASKED ME ALL KINDS OF QUESTIONS, MANY OF WHICH DIDN'T SEEM TO APPLY.

MY ALCOHOL USE? NOT MUCH — TWO OR THREE GLASSES A DAY.

OF COURSE I DRINK ALONE: I'M SINGLE.

SHADES OF HOPE

ON THE SECOND LEG OF THE TRIP THE PLANE HAD ONLY EIGHT SEATS, BUT I WASN'T AFRAID.

TOOK TWENTY MILLIGRAMS OF AMBIEN, DRANK THREE GLASSES OF WINE.

I THOUGHT ABOUT BEN, WHO'D FLOWN TO NEW YORK TO SEE ME THE WEEKEND BEFORE I'D LEFT.

OK, YOU PROBABLY TAKE A LITTLE TOO MUCH AMBIEN. BUT *REHAB?*

DO YOU KNOW HOW MANY TIMES I'VE TAKEN AMBIEN AROUND YOU? I WAS ON IT ALMOST EVERY TIME WE HAD SEX!

I'D BEEN ALLOWED TO GET AWAY WITH ANYTHING, BECAUSE BEN DIDN'T QUESTION A THING THAT I DID. FEAR OF LOSING MY LOVE HAD KEPT HIM SILENT AND COMPLIANT.

SOMETIMES YOU WERE A BIT OUT OF IT, BUT OUR SEX LIFE WAS GREAT.

I WASN'T THERE. EVER.

A WOMAN MET ME AT THE AIRPORT IN BUFFALO GAP. SHE COULD HAVE BEEN ONE OF MY SORORITY SISTERS.

WELL, **HI** THERE!

HI.

SHE CHATTERED ALL THE WAY TO SHADES OF HOPE. I WAS TOO OUT OF IT TO ASK HER WHAT TO EXPECT.

FIFTEEN MINUTES LATER, WE ARRIVED. IT DIDN'T LOOK LIKE THE TYPE OF PLACE ASHLEY JUDD WOULD REST HER HEAD.

THIS IS IT?

YEP, THIS IS HOME!

ASHLEY HADN'T MENTIONED ANY OF THIS. WHERE WERE THE PRETTY OAK TREES? THE YOGA STUDIO?

I DIDN'T SEE THE SERENITY GARDEN.

OH, YOU WON'T SEE **THAT** FOR A WHILE. YOU'RE ON GENERAL MONITOR — SO YOU CAN'T LEAVE THE FRONT PORCH OF THE HOUSE.

WHAT'S GENERAL MONITOR?

SO MANY QUESTIONS! WAIT RIGHT HERE, AND I'LL BRING YOU DINNER.

I ALREADY ATE.

BETTER GET HUNGRY, THEN!

I ATE HALF OF THE DINNER SHE SERVED AND PUSHED THE REST AWAY.

I DON'T LIKE FISH.

WE DON'T DO "HATE FOODS" HERE.

POKE

POKE

POKE

LATER THAT NIGHT, I WAS SHOWN TO MY ROOM.

YOU'RE NOT IN THE DORMS? LUCKY!

MY ROOMMATES:

HI, I'M PAMELA.

PAMELA WAS FORTY-EIGHT AND AN ALCOHOLIC. IT WAS HER FIRST NIGHT THERE TOO.

RACHEL WAS A RAGEAHOLIC. HER HUSBAND HAD INSISTED SHE GET TREATMENT AFTER SHE THREW A LAMP AT HIS HEAD.

WHERE'S THE SPA IN THIS DUMP?!

JANELLE, A COMPULSIVE OVEREATER, WEIGHED AT LEAST FOUR HUNDRED POUNDS. SHE NEEDED ASSISTANCE IN ORDER TO SHOWER.

I COULDN'T SEE HOW I FIT IN WITH THAT MOTLEY CREW. IN FACT, I WAS DETERMINED NOT TO.

SO WHAT'S YOUR POISON? ALCOHOL? PILLS? FOOD?

I DON'T KNOW.

AT 9:30 PM, WE LINED UP OUTSIDE THE NURSE'S OFFICE TO GET OUR MEDS. THE NURSE REFUSED TO GIVE ME AMBIEN.

BUT I'M SUPPOSED TO BE TAPERED OFF THE STUFF! I CAN'T JUST STOP COLD TURKEY!

THERE'S NO NOTE FROM MY SUPERVISOR, SO I CAN'T GIVE IT TO YOU.

BUT I WON'T SLEEP A **WINK** TONIGHT!

I DIDN'T.

"GENERAL MONITOR," IT TURNED OUT, MEANT I WAS CONFINED TO A SMALL AREA OF THE PREMISES.

I WAS ALSO ON "TABLE MONITOR"— I HAD TO EAT WITH TECHS, PEOPLE HIRED TO WATCH US.

AND "BATHROOM MONITOR," WHICH MEANT I HAD TO COUNT OUT LOUD WHILE ON THE TOILET, SO COUNSELORS COULD BE CERTAIN I WASN'T THROWING UP.

MOST OF OUR DAY WAS SPENT IN A SINGLE ROOM.

THE CLOSE QUARTERS CREATED FRICTION.

LISA, MICHELLE WON'T STOP STARING AT ME!

WHICH, I LATER LEARNED, WAS EXACTLY WHAT THE COUNSELORS WANTED.

TAKE IT TO GROUP.

THE PLACE WAS **NOTHING** LIKE WHAT I EXPECTED.

ON-SITE MASSEUSE

TOKEN CELEBRITY

THINK THINK THINK

HOT GUY TO MAKE OUT WITH.

DARE TO BE DIFFERE

AT THE SAME TIME, THE RIGOROUS ROUTINE AND STRICT RULES WERE GOOD FOR ME. I WAS LEARNING TO SURRENDER BECAUSE I HAD NO CHOICE.

I KNOW I DRINK **OFTEN**, BUT I DON'T DRINK **A LOT**.

ALL IT TAKES IS THAT FIRST DRINK. NO ONE EVER GOT RUN OVER BY A TRAIN'S CABOOSE.

213

INSTEAD OF ACTING OUT ON OUR ADDICTIONS, WE WROTE. I WROTE A HISTORY OF MY AMBIEN ABUSE, A HISTORY OF MY LOVE ADDICTIONS, A LIST OF MY FATHER'S TRANSGRESSIONS, DETAILS ABOUT MY SEX LIFE. . . . *EVERYTHING.*

I QUICKLY BECAME THE DOSTOYEVSKY OF RECOVERY, DEDICATING HUNDREDS OF PAGES TO MY ISSUES. (I HAD SO MANY OF THEM, AFTER ALL.)

OW.

THE REST OF MY TIME WAS SPENT IN GROUP THERAPY.

NAMES, CLAIMS, AND FEELINGS?

THOSE AREN'T **FEELINGS**, PEOPLE!

BORED.

ITCHY.

FULL.

ONCE A WEEK, THEY BUSSED US TO OUTSIDE AA MEETINGS.

S'THIS WEEKEND, I GEARED UP MY TRUCK AND TOOK HER TO DALLAS.

I FELT ALMOST HUMAN IN THOSE MEETINGS, LISTENING TO PEOPLE TALK ABOUT THEIR LIVES.

SOON, I BEGAN TO SEE TINY, BUT NOTICEABLE CHANGES TAKING PLACE IN MYSELF.

OOH, PAMELA, THIS ONE IS FOR YOU. "'NO' IS A COMPLETE SENTENCE."

GOOD ONE.

AT TIMES WE HAD BREAKOUT, UNEXPECTED FUN.

TEN SPLENDA PACKETS!

ON THE TWELFTH DAY OF REEEHAB, MY TRUE LOVE GAVE TO ME...

TWELVE CONFRONTATIONS!

ELEVEN COUNSELORS YELLING!

215

UNLESS SOMEONE RUINED IT FOR THE WHOLE GROUP.

TINA, YOU'RE LATE. I DON'T SEE A SATURDAY RECOVERY MOVIE IN THIS GROUP'S FUTURE.

BUT WE'RE SUPPOSED TO SEE **28 DAYS**!

I STARTED TO EXPERIMENT WITH PRAYER.

DIE-HARD, LIFELONG ATHEIST

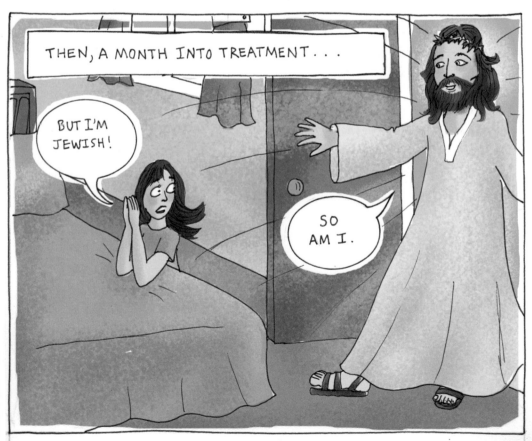

THEN, A MONTH INTO TREATMENT . . .

BUT I'M JEWISH!

SO AM I.

OK, IT DIDN'T EXACTLY HAPPEN LIKE THAT. BUT AFTER A WHILE, I **DID** START TO FEEL A SPIRITUAL CONNECTION TO SOMETHING — NATURE, A HIGHER POWER, CALL IT WHAT YOU WILL. IT WAS SOMETHING GREATER THAN MY FATHER AND GREATER THAN ME.

I DIDN'T FEEL ANXIOUS; I WASN'T OBSESSING ABOUT BEN; AND I WAS SLEEPING SOUNDLY WITHOUT DRUGS FOR THE FIRST TIME IN A DECADE.

IN GROUP THERAPY SESSIONS, THE COUNSELORS STARTED PUSHING ME TO BREAK UP WITH BEN.

YOU'VE SAID YOU FEEL AMBIVALENT ABOUT HIM AND THAT HE DOESN'T SUPPORT YOU IN YOUR RECOVERY.

I SAID HE DOESN'T THINK I NEED IT.

THEY EVEN SUGGESTED I THROW OUT MY TABLOIDS.

MUST I GIVE UP **EVERYTHING** THAT MEANS **ANYTHING** TO ME?

IT'S ANOTHER WAY TO AVOID DEALING WITH YOUR FEELINGS.

EACH WEEK, WE WERE ALLOWED TWO SUPERVISED PHONE CALLS. I CALLED BEN ON THE SLY — I DIDN'T WANT ANYONE LISTENING IN ON US.

IT'S LIKE BOOT CAMP HERE!

OH MY GOD. I WOULDN'T SURVIVE ONE MINUTE. I MISS YOU.

I MISSED HIM TOO. BEN WAS THE FIRST PERSON I'D EVER KNOWN WHO'D LOVED ME UNCONDITIONALLY.

I'LL BE FLYING TO THE EAST COAST ON THURSDAY. I WISH THAT I COULD PARACHUTE INTO YOUR BED.

AND YET, THERE WERE CERTAIN THINGS I COULDN'T TALK TO HIM ABOUT.

IT'S COOL, THOUGH. I'M LEARNING ABOUT SOME INTERESTING THINGS LIKE, UM, GOD.

GOD?!

I COULDN'T HELP BUT THINK ABOUT SOMETHING HE'D SAID IN A TENDER MOMENT WE'D HAD, THE WEEKEND BEFORE I'D LEFT FOR SHADES.

I'M AFRAID YOU'RE GOING TO GROW SO MUCH, YOU'RE NOT GOING TO WANT TO BE WITH ME ANYMORE.

EVEN THEN, I'D SUSPECTED HE WAS RIGHT.

219

FAMILY WEEK

I HAVE A SURPRISE FOR YOU. YOUR FAMILY IS COMING FOR FAMILY WEEK. YEP— EVEN YOUR DAD.

YOU'RE KIDDING.

ONLY MY SISTER KARYN COULDN'T COME. SHE HAD YEAR-OLD TRIPLETS.

DURING FAMILY WEEK, RELATIVES WERE INVITED TO BUFFALO GAP TO PARTICIPATE IN THEIR LOVED ONE'S TREATMENT.

OR, ON OCCASION, IN THEIR NEMESIS'S TREATMENT.

WHAT'S WRONG?

DO YOU THINK I WANT TO BE HERE?

THAT AFTERNOON, WE MET FOR GROUP LECTURES ON CODEPENDENCE AND ALCOHOLISM. FAMILY MEMBERS WERE INSTRUCTED TO SIT SEPARATELY.

BUT IF I SAY NO, MY FAMILY MAKES ME FEEL GUILTY.

NO ONE CAN MAKE YOU FEEL ANYTHING WITHOUT YOUR CONSENT.

THE TIME BEFORE THAT, WE'D BEEN GATHERED IN A HOSPITAL ROOM JUST BEFORE KARYN GAVE BIRTH.

IT OCCURRED TO ME THAT MY FATHER WAS PERPETUALLY FURIOUS, AND IT MIGHT NOT HAVE ANYTHING TO DO WITH ME.

NOR WAS IT MY JOB TO FIX IT.

ON THE SECOND DAY OF FAMILY WEEK, WE HAD READINGS. I SHARED EVERY SINGLE PIECE OF WRITING I'D DONE AT SHADES.

I HAD LITTLE TROUBLE EXECUTING JEREMY'S BIZARRE AND OFTEN UPSETTING REQUESTS, BUT THEN, I'D BEEN PRACTICING S AND M ALL MY LIFE. ONE MINUTE MY FATHER WAS SHOWERING ME WITH LOVE, THE NEXT HE WAS SCREAMING AT ME. IN A WAY, JEREMY AND I WERE A PERFECT FIT.

FINALLY, I WAS PURGING MY SECRETS, IN FRONT OF THE MAN WHO REFUSED TO GIVE UP HIS.

THEN I SPOKE TO WALTER MATHESON — IT TURNED OUT DAD HAD MET HIM AT A MALL AND ASKED FOR THIRTEEN THOUSAND DOLLARS.

WHEN I FINISHED, MY FAMILY WAS ALLOWED TO GIVE FEEDBACK.

NO ANALYSIS, CRITICISM, OR JUDGMENT — JUST "I SAW, I HEARD, I FELT."

IT'S OUTRAGEOUS... TO HAVE TO LISTEN TO THIS — THIS —

BUT IS IT *TRUE?*

YES.

MOM, DO YOU WANT TO GO NEXT?

I HEARD THAT WHEN SHE WAS YOUNG, SHE DIDN'T FEEL I PROTECTED HER. I FELT... PAIN.

FOR THE FIRST TIME, I SAW REAL FEAR ON MY FATHER'S FACE. AND MY MOTHER WASN'T RUSHING TO MAKE IT BETTER.

SO, WHAT — ARE YOU GOING TO LEAVE ME?

DAY FOUR WAS FOR GIVING AND RECEIVING CONFRONTATIONS—
BASICALLY A HIGHLY STRUCTURED WAY TO SAY, "FUCK YOU."

THE ONLY APPROPRIATE RESPONSE TO A CONFRONTATION IS "THANK YOU."

FIRST, MY FATHER GAVE ME HIS.

THANK YOU.

WHEN YOU TOLD THE FAMILY ABOUT MY DEGREES, I THINK YOU BETRAYED ME, AND I FELT **EXTREME** RAGE.

I CONFRONTED HIM ABOUT TAKING OUT CREDIT CARDS IN MY NAME, RAGING AT ME, AND HIS NUMEROUS LIES. IT FELT GOOD TO SAY THOSE THINGS ALOUD AND TO HAVE THEM VALIDATED — IF BEGRUDGINGLY.

THANK YOU.

THE LAST DAY OF FAMILY WEEK WAS RESERVED FOR "LOVES, LIKES, AND FORGIVENESSES." WHEN THE TIME CAME TO FORGIVE MY FATHER, I BASICALLY FAKED IT.

UM, I LOVE YOUR IMAGINATION... AND YOUR GRANDIOSI—GENEROSITY.

THEN IT WAS MY FATHER'S TURN TO READ TO ME.

I LOVE YOUR OUTSIZED TALENT...YOUR SPIRIT... THE FACT THAT YOUR FRIENDS LOVE YOU SO MUCH.

PERHAPS HE'D HAD A CHANGE OF HEART BECAUSE HE WAS ABOUT TO BE EMANCIPATED?

OR MAYBE IT WAS JUST A SHOW. OVER HIS SHOULDER, I GLIMPSED THE FACES SURROUNDING US; THEY WERE SHINY WITH EMOTION.

EVERYONE IN THE **ROOM** WAS CRYING. I WANTED TO FEEL LIKE THEY DID, BUT I COULDN'T. AFTER YEARS OF LEARNING HOW NOT TO BELIEVE MY FATHER, I'D SUCCEEDED.

DID I PLAN TO LIVE THE REST OF MY LIFE AS A BITTER, ANGRY WOMAN-CHILD, PERPETUALLY SEEKING ANSWERS FOR THE CRIMES OF MY CHILDHOOD, OR WAS I GOING TO LET IT GO?

I WANTED TO LET IT GO. I **NEEDED** TO LET IT GO. IN THAT MOMENT, THAT MEANT TAKING MY FATHER'S RESPONSE AT FACE VALUE.

IT MEANT ACCEPTING HIM FOR WHO HE WAS, THEN AND NOW. IT MEANT REALIZING IT DIDN'T MATTER WHAT HIS MOTIVATIONS WERE, AS LONG AS I DIDN'T ALLOW HIM TO CONTINUE TO HURT ME.

PRETENDING ACTUALLY WORKED.

MY FAMILY HAD AN EARLY FLIGHT TO CATCH, SO AN HOUR LATER, WE WERE SAYING OUR GOOD-BYES.

THANK YOU FOR COMING. I KNOW YOU DIDN'T WANT TO.

I LOVE YOU, DARLING. I'M SORRY. I LOVE YOU.

AS I WATCHED THEM DRIVE AWAY, I PICTURED WHAT LIFE WOULD BE LIKE WHEN I GOT OUT. MY MOTHER WOULD GO TO RECOVERY MEETINGS FOR CODEPENDENCE. MY FATHER AND I WOULD SETTLE INTO A NEW KIND OF RELATIONSHIP — ONE WE'D BE FORGING FROM SCRATCH. MY SISTERS AND I WOULD RELATE TO EACH OTHER AS REAL ADULTS. MAYBE WE'D EVEN TALK ABOUT MUNDANE THINGS LIKE THE WEATHER.

SHADES OF HOPE
TREATMENT CENTER

I HOPED, I HOPED.

SHADES OF BROOKLYN

DECEMBER 24, 2006

NEVER HAD I BEEN SO HAPPY TO SEE MY APARTMENT. IT WAS CLEAN, LOVELY, AND MUCH BIGGER THAN I REMEMBERED.

SYLVIE AND MY MOTHER HAD CLEANED OUT MY LIQUOR CABINET, FLUSHED MY LAST BOTTLE OF AMBIEN, AND HAD EVEN TOSSED MY BELOVED TABLOID COLLECTION.

I CALLED BEN. HEARING HIS VOICE WAS BOTH COMFORTING AND STRANGELY DISTURBING.

HEYYY, WELCOME HOME.

WE CHATTED FOR A FEW AWKWARD MINUTES. I'D REFUSED TO BREAK UP WITH BEN IN TREATMENT. I WANTED TO SEE HIM AGAIN, THROUGH SOBER EYES.

THE MOVIE IS GOING WELL. IT LOOKS LIKE WE'RE GOING TO SCREEN IT FOR EXECS ON THE SIXTEENTH. HOW ARE YOU?

I'M REALLY GREAT. THANKS FOR ASKING.

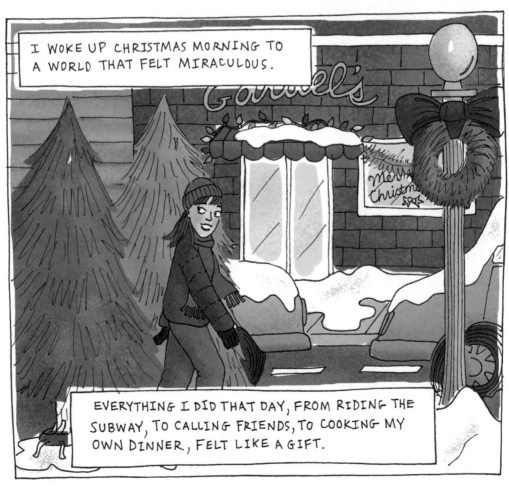

I WOKE UP CHRISTMAS MORNING TO A WORLD THAT FELT MIRACULOUS.

EVERYTHING I DID THAT DAY, FROM RIDING THE SUBWAY, TO CALLING FRIENDS, TO COOKING MY OWN DINNER, FELT LIKE A GIFT.

IT WAS A FEELING I KNEW WOULDN'T LAST. BUT I WANTED TO HOLD ON TO IT FOR AS LONG AS I POSSIBLY COULD.

OVER THE NEXT FEW WEEKS, BEN AND I GOT TO KNOW EACH OTHER AGAIN. WE MAINTAINED A LIGHT, CAREFUL RAPPORT.

WHAT ARE YOU DOING TONIGHT?

I'M MAKING DINNER FOR GENEVIEVE AND TED: VEGETABLE LASAGNA AND SALAD. I LOVE TO COOK NOW!

AND WHILE IT WAS COMFORTING TO HEAR HIS VOICE, I COULDN'T LET HIM IN ON THE CHANGES I WAS GOING THROUGH.

IT WAS A PROCESS I WAS STILL STRUGGLING WITH. I'D BEEN A LIFELONG, DEVOUT ATHEIST. RELIGIOUS-SPEAK HAD ALWAYS SOUNDED TO ME LIKE HUCKSTERISM.

WHAT AM I **DOING?**

BEN AND I HAD BONDED OVER OUR MUTUAL DISDAIN OF THE SUBJECT ON MANY OCCASIONS.

I'D LIKE TO THANK GOD...

YEAH, GOD WAS TOO BUSY INFLUENCING THAT CASTING DIRECTOR TO WORRY ABOUT THE TSUNAMI.

AND YET, UNDENIABLY, THE MORE I GOT DOWN ON MY KNEES, THE MORE I TALKED TO GOD IN THE SHOWER, THE MORE I SURRENDERED TO THE IDEA OF UNCONDITIONAL LOVE (BOYFRIEND OR NO BOYFRIEND, FATHER OR NO FATHER), THE MORE I ACCEPTED MY CIRCUMSTANCES EXACTLY AS THEY WERE...

THE MORE I FELT TAKEN CARE OF, IN A WAY I'D NEVER BEFORE EXPERIENCED. I DIDN'T KNOW WHERE IT WAS GOING, OR IF IT WOULD STICK: I WAS ALL TOO AWARE OF MY TENDENCY TO DIVE HEADFIRST INTO THE IDEA DU JOUR. BUT I WANTED TO TRY IT.

After all, there'd been something standing in the way the whole time: a higher power of my own making.

It was time to give that up. And I didn't want Ben to mock me for throwing myself into recovery.

MEETING IS DOWNSTAIRS AT 7:00 P.M.

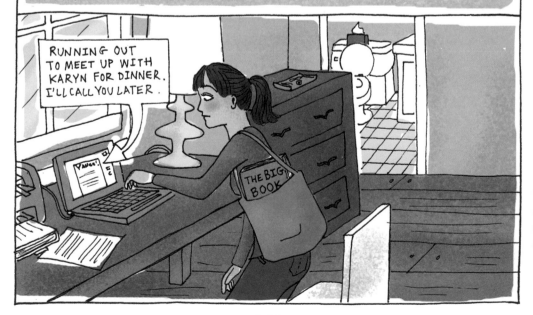

Or to drag me backwards into skepticism, cynicism, and doubt. So I remained silent and didn't let him in.

RUNNING OUT TO MEET UP WITH KARYN FOR DINNER. I'LL CALL YOU LATER.

THE BIG BOOK

BY THE TIME I FLEW TO L.A. AGAIN, THE GULF BETWEEN US HAD WIDENED. WE SAT AT DINNER MAKING SMALL TALK, BEN DRINKING WATER IN SOLIDARITY WITH ME. THE THINGS WE'D ALWAYS TALKED ABOUT TO COVER UP OUR PROBLEMS — BOOKS, MOVIES, CELEBRITIES, OUR FRIENDS — FAILED TO PROVIDE THEIR USUAL SMOKE SCREEN.

OH, AND DEB AND RYAN BROKE UP.

WOW, REALLY?

THE THINGS WE *NEVER* TALKED ABOUT — MY DISSATISFACTION WITH THE RELATIONSHIP, HIS AMBIVALENCE ABOUT CHILDREN, OUR INTIMACY FEARS — REMAINED BURIED.

YEAH, AND HE'S ALREADY DATING SOMEONE ELSE; THIS CUTE BLONDE GIRL.

THAT WAS FAST.

I FELT MY HEART BREAKING AS I LOOKED AT HIM ACROSS THE TABLE. HE WAS A GOOD GUY WHO LOVED ME, BUT IF I STAYED WITH HIM, I COULDN'T GROW. BY THE TIME THAT FIRST NIGHT WAS UP, I KNEW I HAD TO BREAK UP WITH HIM FOR GOOD.

237

IT TOOK ME A FEW DAYS TO WORK UP THE NERVE TO TELL HIM. AND I STILL DIDN'T DO IT VERY ELOQUENTLY.

WE ENDED EVERY BREAKUP CONVERSATION THIS WAY. I COULDN'T SAY THE WORDS "IT'S OVER," AND HE COULDN'T HEAR THEM.

LET'S JUST...NOT TALK FOR A WHILE.

GOOD-BYE FOR NOW.

FOR NOW.

BUT THIS TIME, IT REALLY WAS OVER.

THAT WAS THE LAST TIME I EVER SAW HIM.

THE GOOD LIFE

I WAS GOING TO YOGA AGAIN AND ATTENDING REGULAR RECOVERY MEETINGS. THE MAGAZINE I WORKED FOR OFFERED ME A CONTRACT, WHICH MEANT I WAS ABLE TO WORK FROM HOME. I'D GOTTEN A DOG, A LITTLE TEN-POUND RESCUE NAMED VIOLET. LIFE WAS GOOD.

WHO COULD THROW YOU AWAY? LOOK AT YOU!

THOUGH MY NEW LIFE APPROX-IMATED THE OLD ONE, NOTHING ABOUT IT FELT THE SAME.

GOING TO SLEEP WAS DIFFERENT.

SPENDING TIME WITH MY MOTHER WAS DIFFERENT.

OLD MACDONALD HAD A FARM...

239

INTERVIEWING CELEBRITIES WAS DIFFERENT. THE SUBJECT OF MY FATHER NEVER CAME UP, AND STILL I WAS ABLE TO DRAW THEM OUT.

EVERYTHING WAS DIFFERENT.

AND YET THERE WAS ONE THING THAT HADN'T CHANGED.

THANKSGIVING 2007

THE MINUTE I WALKED INTO MY AUNT'S CONDO, I SPOTTED MY FATHER. IT WAS HIS ISOLATION THAT MADE HIM SO NOTICEABLE.

LAURIE'S HERE!

241

I GAVE UP.

YOU'RE VERY ADORABLE, AREN'T YOU?

THE BIRD IS SERVED!

I KNEW THEN I WAS NEVER GOING TO HAVE A FATHER WHO WOULD ASK ME HOW I WAS DOING, LISTEN TO MY OPINIONS, OR WORRY ABOUT MY EMOTIONAL WELL-BEING. HE'D NEVER DONE ANY OF THOSE THINGS, ANYWAY, BUT I'D NEVER LOST HOPE THAT HE MIGHT. ALL THAT WAS GOOD IN MY FATHER WAS NOW CLOSED OFF TO ME TOO.

YOU SHOULD HAVE **SEEN** THE DINNERS AT MY AUNT'S HOUSE: EVERYBODY SCATTERED IN, AND THEY'D COOK FORTY CHICKENS, THREE OR FOUR ROASTS, THIRTY GALLONS OF SOUP, TWENTY PIES — THERE MUST HAVE BEEN ONE HUNDRED LOAVES OF BREAD — YOU ATE LIKE A HORSE! YOU SAT DOWN TO EAT AT ONE PM AND FINISHED AT FIVE IN THE AFTERNOON. IT WAS **WONDERFUL.**

NOR WOULD I EVER HAVE A MOTHER WHO WOULD ATTEND RECOVERY MEETINGS, AS I'D IMAGINED SHE MIGHT ON THAT LAST DAY AT SHADES.

VRRRROOOM!

OR SISTERS WHO HAD ANY DESIRE TO CONFRONT MY FATHER AND FORCE A FAMILY TRUTH. THEY'D LONG SINCE FORGIVEN HIS TRANSGRESSIONS.

SOUNDS BETTER THAN THE THANKSGIVING DINNERS YOU HAD IN VIETNAM.

UGH, GROSS.

NONE OF THAT MATTERED ANYMORE. I KNEW WHAT I HAD TO DO.

CALL A BIT MORE OFTEN, OK?

IT HAD COST MY FAMILY TOO MUCH TO LIVE IN THEIR FICTIONS. I WASN'T WILLING TO PAY THE SAME PRICE.

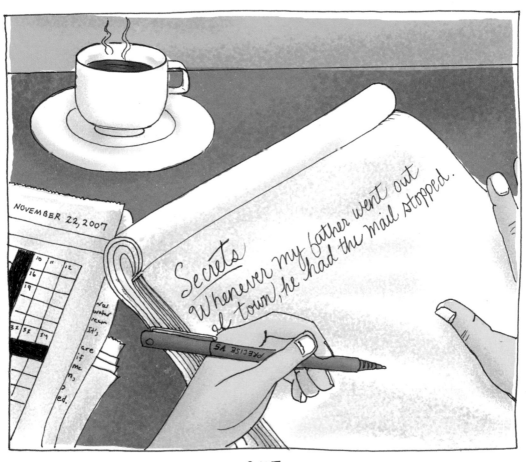

NOVEMBER 22, 2007

Secrets

Whenever my father went out of town, he had the mail stopped.

EACH OF THE BRILLIANT PEOPLE PICTURED BELOW — FROM MY AGENT AT
AND HER TALENTED ASSISTANT, NATHAN ROSTRON, TO THE INCOMPARABLE
EDITED NUMEROUS EARLY DRAFTS AND LENT HER EXPERTISE
SUPPORTIVE FRIENDS — CONTRIBUTED TO THIS BOOK IN
WOULD NOT EXIST. (OK, IT MIGHT EXIST, BUT IT

MY HEARTFELT THANKS TO, FROM LEFT TO RIGHT (FIRST ROW): FIONA MAAZEL,
JESSIE WICK, NATHAN ENGLANDER, CAROLE RADZIWILL; (SECOND ROW)
NATHAN ROSTRON, MERRILL MARKOE, PAIGE POOLER, ASHLEY JUDD,
ROBERTSON, LESLIE ROBARGE, JILL HERZIG, MARYELLEN GORDON,
GELERNTER, DEREK LOOSVELT, MELISSA BELLINELLI; (FOURTH
BROWER, KRISTAN SAKS, STACEY PLATT, PATRICIA COLLINS, ABIGAIL
MARVIN, TANYA ASNES, ROBERT WILKINS. I ALSO THANK SHADES
THE CORPORATION OF YADDO, AND EDDIE STERN, RESPECTIVELY,
IN, AND TEACHING ME HOW TO BREATHE. I OWE A HUGE DEBT OF
TO MY MOTHER, FOR LOVING ME NO MATTER WHAT. FINALLY,
INSPIRED ME TO PICK UP THE PEN. I REMAIN IN AWE OF

246

ICM, AMANDA URBAN, TO MY EDITOR AT LITTLE, BROWN, JUDY CLAIN,
PAIGE POOLER, WHO DID THE COLOR, TO GENEVIEVE FIELD, WHO
THROUGHOUT EVERY STEP OF THE PROCESS, TO MY AMAZINGLY
ONE CRUCIAL WAY OR ANOTHER. WITHOUT THEM, THIS BOOK
WOULD BE A LOT LESS AWESOME.)

ANDY WARD, JENNY ROSENSTRACH, MY SISTERS KARYN AND SYLVIE,
JUDY CLAIN, AMANDA URBAN, GENEVIEVE FIELD, CINDI LEIVE,
AMANDA STERN; (THIRD ROW) AL MCEVOY, ARIEL FOXMAN, PAUL
ROB TOURTELOT, KAREN RAMOS, JOANNA BOBER, MELISSA
ROW) DANA CLORFENE, STEPH CORRADO, ALISSA QUART, ALISON
PESTA, TOM KEALEY, JENNIFER GISTRAK, KYLE SPENCER, CATE
OF HOPE TREATMENT CENTER, BLUE MOUNTAIN CENTER AND
FOR SAVING MY LIFE, GIVING ME BEAUTIFUL SPACES TO WORK
GRATITUDE TO "BEN," FOR HIS UNCONDITIONAL SUPPORT, AND
I WOULD LIKE TO ACKNOWLEDGE MY FATHER, WHO FIRST
HIS MYRIAD GIFTS.

About the Author

Laurie Sandell is a contributing editor at *Glamour*, where she writes cover stories, features, and personal essays. She has also written for *Esquire, GQ, New York,* and *In Style,* among other publications. In her twenties, she spent four years traveling around the world, having unsavory experiences she later justified as "material."